D1165545

INTRODUCTION
TO UTOPIA

INTRODUCTION TO UTOPIA

By

HENRY W. DONNER

Select Bibliographies Reprint Series

BOOKS FOR LIBRARIES PRESS
FREEPORT, NEW YORK

CHABOT COLLEGE LIBRARY

HAYWARD, CALIFORNIA

HX
811
1576
25D6

All Rights Reserved Sidgwick & Jackson 1946

Reprinted 1969 by Arrangement

STANDARD BOOK NUMBER:

8369-5042-9

LIBRARY OF CONGRESS CATALOG CARD NUMBER:

78-94268

PRINTED IN THE UNITED STATES OF AMERICA

To the Memory of
Raymond Wilson Chambers

62739

PREFATORY NOTE

The *Utopia* of St. Thomas More possesses an exceptional interest for us to-day, inasmuch as the problems facing its author were not unlike our own. Incessant wars, unemployment and poverty, the undermining of authority, the lack of morals and religion; — these were some of his problems. The political and social history of Europe since More's day has confirmed his solution in many instances, and it would be presumption to ignore it in others. For More was a man who, in the words of the late Gilbert Chesterton, written some fifteen years ago, »is more important at this moment than at any moment since his death, even perhaps the great moment of his dying; but he is not quite as important as he will be in about a hundred years time. He may come to be counted the greatest Englishman, or at least the greatest historical character in English history.» But in order to benefit fully from his example, we must attempt to understand him.

The present essay, being a revision of a lecture delivered to the *Nyfilologiska Sällskapet* at *Stockholms Högskola* in 1942 and here reprinted from the *Studier i modern språkvetenskap*, is designed as an introduction to the study of one of his most important works, *Utopia; or, the best state of a public weal*. Socialists have seen in it a strong plea for communism. German scholars have imputed to it the beginnings of British imperialism. Roman Catholics regard it as »a picture of the state of society to which man can attain without revelation». After the brilliant exposition of the meaning of *Utopia*, given by the late R. W. Chambers, to whose memory the present work is inscribed in veneration and humility, there can be little doubt about the essential correctness of the third interpretation. In view of the persistent misrepresentation of the intention of *Utopia* by German critics, whose method of approach to their subject is illustrated in the Notes, a somewhat fuller and more amply documented statement has nevertheless seemed desirable.

I have much pleasure in acknowleging the assistance of Professor Arvid Gabrielson who has read my work in manuscript, and of Mrs. Margaret Bottrall who has helped me with the revision of the proofs. Many corrections have been introduced, and many mistakes avoided, as a result of Mrs. Bottrall's vigilance and kindness. I also wish to thank the British Council and its former representative in Sweden, Professor Ronald Bottrall, for their kind and generous assistance in obtaining for me numbers of books without which the preparation of this essay would have been impossible in an isolation which at times has been complete. My indebtedness to the British Council is further increased by the help so freely offered by its present representative in Stockholm, Professor Michael Roberts, who has kindly undertaken to get the printed sheets transported to England.

H. W. D.

Stockholm
May 1945

CONTENTS

    I. Utopian metamorphoses   1
   II. *Utopia* and Latin literature   6
  III. The political background   9
   IV. Humanist satire and the tale of travel   15
    V. A Platonic dialogue   18
   VI. Sources   25
  VII. Utopian society   29
 VIII. Foreign policy   39
   IX. Religion   49
    X. European parallels and contrasts   54
   XI. Imperialism?   60
  XII. Communism?   66
 XIII. Solution   75
Notes   84
Index 110

I

»You have no idea how I jump for joy, how tall I have grown,
how I hold up my head, when a vision comes before my eyes,
that my Utopians have made me their perpetual prince!» More
wrote to Erasmus in December 1516.[1] »I seem already to be
marching along, crowned with a diadem of wheat, conspicuous in a
Greyfriars cloak and carrying for sceptre a few ears of corn; sur-
rounded by a noble company of Amaurotians, and with this numerous
attendance meeting the ambassadors and princes of other nations
— poor creatures in comparison with us, inasmuch as they pride
themselves on coming out laden with childish ornaments and woman-
ish finery, bound with chains of that hateful gold, and ridiculous
with gems and other bubbly trifles.

— — —

I was proceeding further with this delightful dream, when the
break of day dispersed the vision, deposing poor me from my
sovereignty and recalling me to prison — that is, to my legal work.
Nevertheless I console myself that real kingdoms are not much
more lasting.»

As earthly kingdoms go Utopia has in fact proved more
lasting than most, perhaps not so much because it was no
kingdom, nor even entirely owing to the fact that it never was
at all, but on account of that suggestive power it possesses as
of something that might have been, or that may be and may at
any moment materialize before our eyes, just as with evident
satisfaction More saw it in his dream. But though we see it
in the mind's eye, and though many have looked forward to it
as to a coming millennium, More had no illusions as to its
being more than a dream. And like a dream, although more

rational than most, it misleads us to believe in all its mocking intricacies, its reality of minutest detail, its concrete vision, its baffling absurdities and contradictions, down to those schizophrene elements which are absent from no dreams. It is only when we start transplanting it into the world which surrounds us, rebuilding it out of mundane matter, that we miss the mortar which should join the bricks together. The stones are there, but the building is a vision; the trees are there, the fields and rivers, but there is no water in them; the country is there, but inhabited by puppets moving on strings pulled by a Socratic stage-manager. It is a country where friends are received as cordially as More would have provided for the reception of Erasmus and Tunstal by his subjects, in spite of his new greatness always mindful of their friendship[1]; but where the proud and vain are laughed to scorn like the Anemolians[2] or those foreign ambassadors, »looking like devils out of hell», whom as a young man More had watched with such amusement when they came escorting the beautiful Princess Catherine through the streets of London[3]. And so More has not escaped the bitter retaliation of some would-be visitors to his principality, and his own ambassadors have not always been received at the courts of worldly princes in that spirit of unruffled good humour in which they were once despatched across uncharted seas.

Utopia has remained a vision, and the very word »Utopian», with which More has enriched all European languages, has come to signify a state »possessing or regarded as having impossibly or extravagantly ideal conditions in respect of politics, customs, social organization, etc.» or else »involving, based or founded on, imaginary or chimerical perfection; impossibly ideal, visionary».[4] In current language an element of wish-fulfilment seems to be commonly associated with the term, regardless of whether the wish be for good or evil.[5] »A noun and an adjective of abuse» Mr. H. G. Wells has cynically called More's contribution to the language[6], but More could only be held responsible for the pejorative sense in which his words are used, if he had himself fallen a victim to the delusion of his dream.

More formed »Utopia» out of the Greek to indicate »Nowhere», as appears from his synonymical use of »Nusquama» in his letters.[1] With grim humour Budé did not hesitate to call it »Udepotia».[2] Yet, if the mansion was a vision, the stones were cut out of the perennial marble, and historians and sociologists have been concerned to show to what a considerable extent More's far-sighted provisions for his imaginary Utopians have been copied by modern legislators, while some of them remain the very practicable aims of present day social policy.[3]

In the history of political thought, international law and social progress More occupies a prominent place. Latitudinarian theology, Utilitarian philosophy and modern sociology have all received irresistible impulses from Utopia. The conceptions of natural law and natural religion largely owe their rebirth to More's imaginary commonwealth. To his inspiration has been attributed the whole trend of social reform.[4] He introduced compulsory and universal education and complete equality of the sexes in his dreamed republic, he abolished private property and advocated the short working day and the abolition of capital punishment for theft, he influenced the revision of the Poor Laws and inspired the industrial reforms as well as the dreams of Ruskin, Bellamy, Morris and Howells.[5] The entire movement of socialism was, so to speak, born under the star of Utopia. In Utopian communism social reformers have seen an ideal solution of the problems of society, and some of the foremost protagonists of socialism have paid More the compliment of imitation, like Morelly in his *Naufrage des îles flottantes*, Cabet in his *Voyage en Icarie*, and more recently Theodor Hertzka in *Freiland; ein sociales Zukunftbild*. Of those who have advanced the cause of communism in practice more than one has been, like Robert Owen, inspired by More's example in the *Utopia*, which made such an indelible impression also on Marx and Engels.[6] Among his most enthusiastic biographers is found the Marxist Karl Kautsky. And thus it happens that More, who suffered martyrdom in the cause of an undivided Christendom and has been canonized a saint by the Roman Catholic Church, has as the author of *Utopia* been elevated to the Bolshevist hierarchy, and his feast is celebrated in the calendar of the Red Army. His works were forbidden in the Third

Reich, but he became the patron saint of German Catholics suffering persecution for their faith.[1]

Hardly less important has been the literary influence of More's *Utopia*, for if it has been universally recognized as the most far-sighted of ideal commonwealths, it is also the earliest of a long line of political romances or what the Germans call »Staatsromane», and so it claims a double title as the proto-type of an important literary species. As the first since class-ical antiquity it set the fashion for descriptions of ideal com-monwealths, whether directly inspired by its example, like Campanella's *Civitas solis* and Francis Bacon's *New Atlantis*, or written for a philosophical or political purpose, like Thomas Hobbes' *Leviathan* or James Harrington's *Oceana*, not to men-tion a great number of similar productions of earlier and later dates. Whether founded on contemporary and universal ex-perience, like Swift's *Gulliver*, or returning to the allegiance of Plato, like Bulwer-Lytton's *The Coming Race*, Utopian fancies have rarely escaped the mark of their Morian origin.

However numerous its offspring in a direct line of descent, the bar sinister has not concealed the ancestry of a motley crowd of bastards also deriving from the fertile womb of the Utopian republic. The influence of *Utopia* has been by no means limited to political romances proper. It pervades a great number of fantastic tales of travel also, of the type of *Robinson Crusoe,* which, like *Gulliver*, borrowed from *Utopia* both the element of social criticism and that circumstantial method of description to which it owes its convincing verisimilitude. And so More has become the father of a species of literature whose mere headings fill vast bibliographies.[2] Nor has the source of Anyder run dry, and since the French Revolution no period has been richer in Utopian experiments than our own. Suffice it to men-tion on the one hand works of such widely different aim and character as Mr. H. G. Wells's *A Modern Utopia* and Mr. Aldous Huxley's *Brave New World*, and on the other Miss Rose Mac-auley's *Orphan Island* and M. René Puaux's *La grande voyage*. Even in Scandinavia the Utopian trend is represented by works of such variety as Holberg's *Niels Klim*, Topelius's sketch of *Det landet Victoria* and Strindberg's *De lycksaligas ö*.[3]

The point of the Utopian romance is its implied criticism of society in the description of a commonwealth whose institutions appear ideal by means of the contrast it presents to the conditions actually prevailing. It may be staged in a supposedly unknown and distant part of the world as in More's own book, beyond the oceans or the skies, or in a distant future beyond time as in the works of modern socialists. The conditions of this imaginary country may be frankly represented as ideal, as in Bellamy's *Looking Backward*, or suggest the ideal by means of caricature, as in Butler's *Erewhon*. Neither method is foreign to More.

· A distinction of even greater interest to the present inquiry concerns the author's seriousness of purpose. He may visualize his imaginary republic in a Lucianic revelation, like Cyrano de Bergerac in his Journeys to the Sun and Moon, or, on the other hand, he may create a country such as he himself would like to live in, a coming millennium, where all his dreams come true, where crime and evil have no place, as in William Morris's *News from Nowhere*. Where the emphasis is on entertainment a Robinsonian fancy will usually result, where the desire to reform predominates a *Staatsroman* will commonly ensue. Both elements are present in *Utopia,* but whereas the former makes its presence felt principally in the style, the contents are largely made out of the latter element. It is the extreme complexity of More's work that has confused his critics. Its chief literary influence, from Rabelais to Disraeli, has proceeded from the former, but it is through the latter category that *Utopia* has exercised its most powerful social influence. If, however, later writers have often embodied their political programmes in Utopian fancies, it does not necessarily follow that *Utopia* was intended as an expression of the practical aims of an author who created a combination of methods which has later resulted in a recognized literary species, but who never accepted the limitations of any one manner of approach to a richly faceted subject. If, moreover, many of the Utopian devices have proved practicable and even desirable in modern society, this does not necessarily mean that their inventor, like so many of his successors, regarded them as models worthy of imitation.

To a considerable extent Utopian criticism has been ruled by sociological considerations. Yet the vast literary influence of More's visionary work seems to invite the attention of the literary critic, and it seems reasonable to suspect that its enduring power may be partly an effect of the presence in it of literary qualities, lacking in some of his less successful imitators. Happily the ever increasing importance of More for our own day has resulted in an understanding of the character of *Utopia*, rare even ten or a dozen years ago.

II

The *Utopia* of St. Thomas More belongs to that class of modern Latin literature which has not yet received its full share of critical appreciation. It was written in the years 1515 and 1516 and published by Thierry Martin at Louvain before the end of the latter year under the title *Libellus vere Aureus nec minus salutaris quam festivus de optimo reip. statu deque noua Insula Vtopia*. Barely twelve months later a second edition appeared from the press of Gilles de Gourmont in Paris, and in the course of 1518 two issues, dated March and November respectively, were brought out by the prince of publishers north of the Alps, John Froben, at Basle. The numerous commendatory epistles included, not the names of the unknown young, anxious by means of the newly invented art of printing to live on another's fame, but among many well known humanists the names also of the two foremost scholars of Europe, Guillaume Budé and Desiderius Erasmus. Throughout the sixteenth century new editions continued to be printed at the chief centres of Western civilization, such as Venice, Louvain, Cologne, and Wittenberg, until it was, in Thomas Stapleton's phrase, to be found »in every man's hands».[1] It was translated into German, Italian, French, and Spanish, and finally an English version by Ralph Robynson appeared in 1551.[2] Several translations have been produced since then, but neither the better sense nor the more faithful rendering of the Latin has been able to oust the vigour and quaintness of the Tudor version from the preference it has enjoyed with the English reading public.

In the translation of Ralph Robynson *Utopia* has become an English classic, still rivalling the fame of its more popular successors *Robinson* and *Gulliver*. With the passing of Latin as a universal language it has come to be read and studied in translation more frequently than in the original, and even scholars of literature have evinced a keener interest in its content of political and social ideas than in that humanist Latin language whose problems excite little interest to-day. Yet it was in its original crisp and pregnant form that *Utopia* first gained approval and was received with enthusiasm by all the best wits of Europe, and in the form originally given it by More it still shows to the happiest advantage. Yet it must be admitted that the power of More's thought has forced some fine utterances even from the less elegant pen of Robynson.

A new civilization is more impressionable than an old, and hence it requires greater genius to impress a personal stamp on an old medium and to give it the lure of novelty than to write tolerably in a new language. Nevertheless historians of literature have invariably devoted greater efforts to the elucidation of the early stages of a new civilization than to the analysis of the last throes of an old culture. The vernacular literatures of the Renaissance have consequently received far greater attention than the large body of international Latin, doomed soon to be outshone by her younger sisters. Not that English was a new language when Robynson wrote, but it had been dozing and was only just waking from aureate slumbers. This awakening was very largely a result of the efforts of More and his circle, pioneers of historical, biographical, controversial and dramatic writing. More is recognized as holding one of the most important places in the history of English prose. He did not choose to adopt *Utopia* among his English works, as he did his *History of Richard III*, and it must claim its rank as a work of literature before an international court among the foremost productions of its age. Its real greatness will perhaps become more conspicuous when modern Latin is one day treated on a par with the vernacular literatures of Europe instead of being often overlooked and inadequately regarded as the freak productions of a limited company of the learned. In the meanwhile it must live on the eternal power of its thought, in spite of a form which has now become inaccessible to the majority of the reading public. This form, however, is worthy of a short mention for its own sake.

One of the achievements of humanism was the restoration of a pure Latin prose style. So strict was its canon that scarcely a word or phrase was admitted unless documented in the works of Cicero or Quintilian. Such rigour was perhaps necessary in order to terminate the rule of monkish patois, but the classical manner suffered from a disability to express contemporary thought except by a circumlocution which is one of the most tiresome features of the productions of the humanists. In opposition to the Laurentian tradition, if I may so style the school of Valla, Erasmus was to plead for greater freedom in his *Ciceronianus*. Without ever descending to the Latinized vernacular of the Schoolmen, More ten years earlier had the courage to write a Latin prose which is both freer and more original than that of Petrarch or Erasmus. Latin was to him a living language, capable of development according to the requirements of his age and of a topical subject.

While able and learned annotators have exhaustively dealt with his classical allusions and elucidated his meaning[1], an analysis of More's style was not undertaken until Mme. Marie Delcourt published her edition of the Latin text in 1936[2]. The examination of his vocabulary has resulted in a new light being thrown on the extent of More's reading and his freedom from prejudice where the choice of words is concerned. He disdains neither archaic nor post-classical terms. Poetical words are not unwelcome when they serve his purpose. The use of Plautus and Terence is as conspicuous as it is consonant with the nature of his subject. It is moreover interesting to note that if More treated Latin as a living language, it was nevertheless under his hands a learned language also, capable of demonstrating his knowledge of even the rarest authors.[3] The preference for rare words is so marked, indeed, that Mme. Delcourt has reached the conclusion that where the text is in doubt the less usual form should be accepted by editors for the very reason of its rarity.[4] There was no doubt an element of snobbery in this display of learning, but even more it was an expression of that humanist wit, many manifestations of which are so difficult for us to understand. The very subject chosen, moreover, required the use of a certain number of technical terms which he had to seek where he might find them. For the legal distinctions he had to draw on the Pandects and the Justinian Codex. But he did not refrain from occasionally employing later mediæval terms and borrowing from the Bible and more than one Christian author. Not infrequently he ventured on new formations, such as *populivorus*, formed in analogy with *carnivorus*, and the superb *oligopolium*, in analogy with *monopolium*, which if it had been Anglicized by Robynson into »oligopoly» could hardly have failed to be universally adopted.[1] Occasionally More would translate a Greek term into Latin, and altogether his vocabulary testifies to his resourcefulness.

His writing is often careless and negligent of grammar in the same way in which we usually claim a greater freedom in our own language. More is thoroughly at home in Latin. The very freedom is witness to his mastery. He makes full use of all the liberties taken by Tacitus and even adds considerably to their number.[2] His eliptical phrases and frequent parentheses give the impression of actual speech. To some extent this may be the effect of the hasty composition of the first book, which, as Erasmus tells us, is discernible in the style.[3] Sometimes the thought develops slowly and circumspectly in sentences reminiscent of his English works.[4] His English origin may be spotted also in the preference for certain locutions like the superlative *maxime* plus adjective. Of considerable interest, however, is the admission of his critics that More's free and easy sentences never fail to express his meaning more adequately than a strictly »correct» grammar would permit.[5] Suffice it to say that in the great days when style was still a necessary complement to learning, the author of *Utopia* became recognized as one of the three foremost scholars of Europe.

III

The growing recognition of More's stature has reacted favourably on Utopian criticism and resulted in a revision of numerous misconceptions. Many wise things have been said about *Utopia* by learned annotators[1] and profound scholars[2], and all that seems required in this place seems to be a restatement of some of the chief points with such additional argumentation as may be deemed necessary to meet recent criticism. For it does not seem unreasonable to maintain that out of the likeness of our own age to his we are to-day better qualified to pronounce judgment on More's work than others living at any time since the beginning of the modern era. Like ours, the period in which *Utopia* was written was one of material and social change, of upheavals and war, internecine and external. It was an age marked by the prolonged agony of the passing of the Middle Ages with all their institutions, political and social, their ways and habits both of body and of mind, their geographical limits and their conceptions of the universe, alike the world in which they lived and the world for which they hoped. It was a period of confusion and turmoil where no authority remained unquestioned, whether spiritual or temporal; one of those inevitable relapses which periodically interrupt the progress of civilization and of which we are experiencing one of the gravest at the present day. The full rage of the storm had not yet broken when More wrote his *Utopia* and the book expresses throughout the optimism of its author and the high hopes entertained by the humanists for the peaceful solution of the tangled problems of the day. If it pleads with earnestness it moves to laughter also, and it is often difficult to say which vein prevails. Yet we can say for certain that, if it had been written ten years later, many things expressed in it would have been said differently, if at all; and if More had been able to imagine even in his wildest dreams that it might ever be interpreted in a way likely to undermine authority and subvert society, it would never have been written.[3] As it was, it took shape in that happy interval when »heaven laughed and the earth rejoyced»[4], before that earthquake which was to swallow most of what was good and beautiful in England, and before the fates were yet thirsting for human sacrifice. Yet the faith that was to uphold him on the scaffold was already firmly fixed in the mind of More,

and any interpretation of *Utopia* which proceeds in forgetfulness
of this fact is bound to be misleading.

The topical interest which the *Utopia* possesses for us to-day
centres in its vigorous attack, at the very moment of its
triumph, on that capitalist system which has since then pre-
vailed, but is now crumbling. It was written at a time when,
in Professor A. F. Pollard's phrase, »the mediæval England of
laymen and clerks was merging into the modern England of
rich and poor».[1] Powerful landlords in quest of riches, finding
sheep-farming more profitable than agriculture, were enclosing
the common land to serve as grazing for their sheep, while the
wool went to feed the mills of Flanders. The farmers were
mercilessly driven from their homes and reduced to the choice
of begging their way, enlisting in the troops of mercenaries,
or being hanged for theft. »Forsooth», said More, »your sheep
that were wont to be so meek and tame, and so small eaters,
now . . . be become so great devourers, and so wild, that they
eat up and swallow down the very men themselves.» (This was
a phrase Karl Marx was not to forget.) »They consume, destroy,
and devour whole fields, houses, and cities.»[2] The old economic
system based on manorial self-sufficiency was giving way to the
new method of exchanging goods for money. Feudalism was
dying and the chief nobles, who had been the great land-owners,
lay dead on the fields of battle. At each demise of the crown, so
frequent during the Wars of the Roses, the land of the dead and
of the survivors on the losing side was confiscated and put up for
sale to the highest bidder. It was not until after More's death that,
in consequence of the Reformation, estate jobbing became the
favourite occupation of upstart courtiers and the *nouveaux riches*,
yet before the *Utopia* was written the foundations were already
being laid of that unequal distribution of wealth which has,
until recently, been characteristic of English society. The material
and spiritual values, hitherto accessible to all, became con-
centrated in the hands of a limited few, to the exclusion of
the poor from any share in either. Hence Raphael Hythloday,
(»the teller of idle tales», who had witnessed the Utopians working
for the good of all in a state where nobody was poor, because
he lacked nothing, and nobody was rich, because he possessed

nothing as his own) is made to say that on his return he could see nothing in the states of Europe except a »conspiracy of rich men, procuring their own commodities under the name and title of the commonwealth».[1] And so More makes him ask: »For what justice is this, that a rich goldsmith» (we should say 'banker') »or an usurer, or, to be short, any of them, which either do nothing at all; or else that which they do is such, that it is not very necessary to the commonwealth; should have a pleasant and wealthy living, either by idleness, or by unnecessary business? when in the mean time poor labourers, carters, ironsmiths, carpenters, and ploughmen, by so great and continual toil, as drawing and bearing beasts be scant able to sustain; and again so necessary toil that without it no commonwealth were able to continue and endure one year; do yet get so hard and poor a living, and live so wretched and miserable a life, that the state and condition of the labouring beasts may seem much better and wealthier.»[2]

More was the first of the great humanists to identify himself whole-heartedly with the cause of the poor. Erasmus[3], Budé[4], and above all Vives followed suit[5]. For when the social organization ceased providing for the masses of the people, untold numbers were forced by poverty to beg or steal; but the punishment for loitering was imprisonment, for theft, be it of the most necessary little slice of food, hanging. Sir John Fortescue in his work on *The Governance of England* had proudly pointed to the fact that the number of malefactors yearly executed was so much greater in England than in France, which circumstance he regarded as a proof of the incorruptibility of English justice and of the bolder spirit of her people.[6] Yet even he was not unconscious of the fact that poverty may be the cause of theft and robbery[7], and More maintained that it is society that first makes the thief and then hangs him[8]. This is done though »God commandeth us that we shall not kill».[9] And More makes Hythloday put the case for humanity: »Surely . . . I think it not right nor justice that the loss of money should cause the loss of man's life. For mine opinion is that all the goods in the world are not able to countervail man's life.»[10] Here we shall do well to remember that it was not till the middle of last century that capital punishment for theft was abolished in England, and at this present day it has been reintroduced with unheard-of vigour in Central Europe. More's remedy was as rational as it has proved consistent with the trend of social reform. He suggested that the same punishment of death should not be indiscriminately inflicted regardless of whether a man had committed theft, homicide, or murder, because such a system tended to aggravate crime[1], but that an attempt should rather be made to provide work for vagabonds and thieves and so give them an opportunity of improving and becoming useful members of society[2]. Let there be introduced a law against enclosures of land[3], he admonished; and it is of no little interest to find that although this evil had not yet nearly reached its height, yet Wolsey was not slow to try More's remedy and to stop the conversion of arable land into pasture. In 1517 a commission was appointed to inquire into the circumstances attending all enclosures of land made since 1485, and a decree against them was issued in the following year.[4] Restore agriculture, was More's advice, and rather than sending the wool to Flanders, provide work by manufacturing the cloth at home.[5]

If More was sympathetic to the poor, he was no less severe on the idle rich at whose houses luxury had assumed hitherto unknown proportions and where large troops of idle servants were hardly kept out of mischief as long as their employment lasted and who were good for no useful work when dismissed without notice in case of their own illness or their employer's death.[6] He attacks their monopoly of sheep-farming and the wool trade, blaming it as the cause of the rise in prices.[7] In the interest of justice and a more equitable distribution of wealth he returns to the conclusion of Aristotle and St. Thomas Aquinas that the Prince's honour and safety rest in the prosperity of his people.[8]

Of all the plagues of those troubled times the marauding mercenaries were one of the very worst. Since they were hardly ever regularly paid, the wars were turned into organized plunder, accompanied by well-nigh incredible atrocities, laying waste whole provinces in the process.[9] When peace was concluded these brutalized hordes were let loose on the country like locusts,

leaving nothing but rack and ruin behind. So new wars had
to be arranged to keep them off the native soil. Again More's
medicine is radical. May princes abstain from war and the
conquest of countries they have no time to rule in any case,
and may they devote their powers to the good of their own
people.[1] Raphael Hythloday is here made to tell a story drawn
from the experience of his own extensive travels; and to More
experience was »the very mother and mistress of wisdom».[2]
It had once happened, says Raphael, that the Achorians (»those
without Lebensraum») had been misguided enough to support
the claims of their prince to another kingdom, but once it was
conquered, they found it as troublesome to keep it as ever it
was to get while their own prince was too busy with his two
kingdoms to be well able to rule one. Tired of constant rebell-
ions, wars, internal disturbances and the poverty caused by them,
and dissatisfied with being governed by but half a king, the
Achorians made him choose which of his two realms he preferred;
and so he was forced to give up his hard-gained conquests to
a friend who »shortly after was violently driven out».[3]

These are some of the contemporary problems More refers
to in the first book of *Utopia*. Constitutional treatises, dealing
with the political problems of the day, had been written in England both in Latin and English during the fifteenth century[4],
but while More is certainly carrying on a tradition, he does not
confine himself to an examination of transitory conditions. He
seeks the root of the evil, always looking to essentials, and
reaching conclusions of universal significance. Nor does he any
more than other political writers abstain from reflections of a
general nature on the problems of statecraft, the art of government, the duties of princes and the rights of citizens, in the
manner of the mediæval *specula principis*, whose tradition mingles
with that of the political treatise of a more recent date in the
first book of *Utopia*. This double nature tends to give to More's
work a vitality not possessed by other moralizing treatises of
the period. Altogether it gives a more vivid impression of the
times in which it was written, than any other source that I can
think of. The details of the political background are described
in the first book of *Utopia* with an imagination and a vividness

of detail, equalled by no other recorder of the period, either contemporary or modern, and they are brought home to us in phrases which it is impossible to forget. The truth of its relation is borne out by all the contemporary evidence, but to it we must concede the first place among the sources of our knowledge of the social and political conditions of the day.[1] Erasmus said that More's purpose in writing *Utopia* »was to show whence spring the evils of states: but he modelled it on the British constitution, with which he is thoroughly familiar».[2] Never was purpose better fulfilled. So far from being more favourable, however, the social conditions of many other countries were even more desperate, and More's picture, though unflattering, holds good of more places than England only.[3]

IV

If two literary traditions, flowing into one, help to make it a political document of unparalleled vigour and accuracy, More's *Utopia* is no less remarkable for the form into which its thought was moulded. The Humanist Movement was bold in satire. Sebastian Brandt's *Narrenschiff*, 1494, was the first of a line of brilliant productions. Translations into Latin, French, and Dutch soon followed; and in 1509 two English versions appeared independently, one of which was the famous revision by Alexander Barclay with its pointed adaptation to English conditions. In the same year Erasmus' celebrated pamphlet *Moriae Encomium* or *Laus Stultitiae* was written at More's house in Bucklersbury and dedicated to him. It was published at Paris in 1511. The *Epistolae obscurorum virorum* were printed in two parts in 1515 and 1517. The *Utopia* is inferior to none of these in the sting of its satire. But while the others were content with ridiculing human weaknesses in general, the vices and stupidity of the monks, and the sophisms of the Scholiasts, More's purpose was constructive. His book is not the less entertaining because it possesses a more permanent value, and the wit of his pen became as celebrated as the wisdom of his counsel.[4]

The dialogue according to the model of Plato became a characteristically humanist form of expression, and satire in the form of dialogue had been combined with fantastic tales of travel as long ago as by Lucian, one of More's favourite authors, four of whose dialogues he had himself translated into Latin.[1] More was perhaps not entirely uninfluenced by his example when he set to work on a similar combination.[2] Tales of travel enjoyed an immense popularity in the later Middle Ages, and the fantastic element was equally prominent in the description of men and monsters. The public, lacking both knowledge and criticism, swallowed them whole. »But as for monsters», says More, »because they be no news» Hythloday will not speak of them. »For nothing is more easy to be found, . . . but to find citizens ruled by good and wholesome laws, that is an exceeding rare and hard thing.»[3] It was in the most popular kind of literary entertainment that More found a means of parody and satire. The great geographical discoveries of his age had done nothing to diminish an appetite for which the witty humanist was determined to cater, while they had opened up new possibilities which he was as quick to grasp as to explore. The popular tales of travel provided him with a form which enabled him to turn his political satire into a vivacious romance, by means of which he hoped to catch the ears of the great, although in this he failed as conspicuously as he succeeded in getting posterity with child, so that his book became the ancestor of an untold literary progeny.

As ambassador to Flanders, More relates, he was detained at Bruges while the negitiators on the opposite side departed for Brussels to know their prince's pleasure. More was wiling away the time at Antwerp, when one day after service in the cathedral he saw his friend Peter Giles, town clerk of Antwerp and a gifted young humanist, engrossed in conversation »with a certain stranger, a man well stricken in age, with a black sunburnt face, a long beard, and a cloak cast homely about his shoulders; whom by his favour and apparel forthwith I judged to be a mariner».[4] This was Raphael Hythloday. He was a man who had travelled as widely over the surface of the earth as in the realms of thought. He had been the companion of Amerigo Vespucci on the last three of his four voyages, and was one out of twenty-four who had obtained their captain's permission

to remain in the New World.[1] He preferred Greek to Latin
since his favourite study was the writings of the philosophers,
and in Latin he found little to his taste except some of the
works of Cicero and Seneca. Thus from the outset fact mingles
with fiction, and satire with humanist propaganda.[2] More invited
his friends to accompany him to his house and there, in true
humanist fashion[3], »upon a bench of turves», as Chaucer has
it, the conversation ensued which is related in the book.

In the first part of *Utopia* this conversation turns on European
affairs, illustrated with examples, real and imaginary, fetched
from England and France no less than from Asia and the New
Found Lands in the West. In this manner More, very artistic-
ally[4], little by little prepares the ground for the account of
Utopia which fills the second book. From the small fort on the
east coast of South America, where he and his companions had
been left by Vespucci, Raphael Hythloday had found his way
over land and across the seas after the lapse of many years to
Ceylon and Calicut, from where he had recently returned to his
native Portugal. (Actually it was not till several years after
the publication of *Utopia* that the ship of Magellan first circum-
navigated the globe.[5]) He had sailed in the small native vessels
propelled by means of sails made of rushes or wicker (apparently of the kind still used by the Aimara Indians on Lake
Titicaca[6]). He had taught the inhabitants of those distant shores
the use of the magnetic needle.[7] He had seen many curious
customs, and his favourite study had been the laws and constitutions of the many countries he visited. »But as he marked
many fond and foolish laws in those new found lands, so he
rehearsed many acts and constitutions whereby these our cities,
nations, countries, and Kingdoms may take example, to amend
their faults, enormities and errors.»[8] This is a point which
I wish particularly to emphasize, for I would like to suggest
that in this phrase More has expressed his real intention with
regard to his own fiction. He is neither wholly serious, for
he is out to entertain, nor is it all a joke, as appears from the
bitter satire and occasionally passionate pleading. With characteristic optimism he left it to his readers to decide which parts
of his book were seriously intended and which were spoken

»in sport»[1], believing with his own Utopians »that the truth of the own power would at the last issue out and come to light»[2]. And if some of his readers were deceived, this could only add to his own amusement.[3]

V

When Peter Giles expresses his surprise that Raphael does not now place his wide experience at the service of a prince, in order to gain both preferment for himself and the means to advance the fortunes of his friends and kinsfolk, the answer oı Hythloday is as disarming as it is characteristic. He has long ago divided his worldly fortune between his relatives, and so they can have no further claim on him. — And here we shall do well to remember the example of Pico della Mirandola, whose Life More had himself translated into English[4], and More's own repeated and incessant warnings against too great an attachment to earthly treasure[5]. — Still less could his cousins demand that for their sake Raphael should give himself in bondage to a king.[6] — And again we must remember Pico's beautiful and dignified answer to similar exhortations of his nephew's[7], the anxiety of Erasmus never to fix his allegiance anywhere permanently[8], and More's own reluctance to enter the royal service[9]. The humanist ideal was an existence removed from the tumult of the world and »the trifles of princes».[10] It represents the mediæval monastic tradition tinged with ancient philosophy. — But in the dialogue More comes to the rescue of Peter Giles, using now in his turn another humanist argument in appealing to his sense of duty and public spirit[11], and persuading Raphael that at a prince's court he might without losing his integrity both be given the opportunity and acquire the influence necessary to serve mankind and improve the common lot, even if it were to be done at the cost of his own comfort[12] Yet Hythloday is inexorable, for he has never yet found princes willing to take advice from anybody. »And verily it is naturally given to all men to esteem their own inventions best.»[13]

The ensuing conversation gives occasion to the criticism of the conditions prevailing in Europe, and particularly in England, which fills the greater part of the first book of *Utopia*. For

Hythloday has visited England during the chancellorship of Cardinal Morton, Archbishop of Canterbury, at whose Palace of Lambeth More had in his childhood served as page and attracted the notice of his kindly patron, and it is with evident satisfaction that the author recalls his shrewd wit, his prudence, learning, and experience.[1] No doubt it is More's own observations on which Hythloday is drawing, when he relates how he learned that at the courts of the great no opinion is approved unless it has first been graciously received by the prince himself. Hythloday had made so bold as to suggest that the people should be provided with employment instead of being turned out of their homes and hanged; that the enclosing of arable land should be prohibited and the growth of sheep-folding stopped; that the wool should be manufactured in England instead of being sent to Flanders; that measures should be taken to stop the increase in prices and the consequent impoverishing of the people; that the empty display of the rich should be restricted, the big idle crowds of useless servants and retainers decreased, the mercenaries dismissed from the army and settled in useful occupations; that princes should abstain from increasing their own wealth at the expense of their subjects, uphold the peace, refrain from foreign conquest, and rather devote their efforts to the improvement of their own country and the happiness of their subjects. All very sensible and practicable suggestions, and as little »Utopian» as possible, in the modern sense of the word, and all things which in the second book we shall find realised in Utopia. However, if it had not been for the intercession of the Cardinal on his behalf, the courtiers would not have failed to silence him.[2]

Hythloday had learned then that among a company of courtiers, or cabinet ministers as we should say, set on a certain course of action, it was completely useless trying to voice a different opinion.[3] If the king's councillors were discussing the means of increasing the wealth of the crown and one suggested the depreciation of the currency, another obtaining grants by making a show of war, a third reinforcing obsolete statutes so as to obtain an income from the fines, a fourth advocating prohibitions and monopolies, while a fifth suggested that the judges should be subjected to the king's control so as to secure judgment always in his favour, and all agreed that no abundance, however great, is great enough for a king, who can do no wrong and to whom rightly belongs all the wealth of his people, while poverty in the subjects serves to deprive them of the means and courage to rebel; if they were all agreed about these aims, it would be little use maintaining the contrary opinion.[1] If, then, Hythloday were to declare that the citizens choose the king, not for his benefit, but for their own sake[2], that it is his duty to provide for their safety and prosperity, just as the shepherd has »to feed his sheep rather than himself»[3]; that beggary and hunger make the people rebel; that »verily one man to live in pleasure and wealth, while all others weep and smart for it, that is the part not of a king, but of a jailor»; that he who cannot improve the lives of his subjects except by taking from them both their lives and means of livelihood, does not know how to govern free men; that the king should start with mending his own life[4], remove the occasions of crime, and give the citizens justice; — if Raphael were to speak to this effect, he would only find deaf listeners[5].

Hythloday then chooses an example from recent events in France, but the application to English policy would be near at hand. Suppose he were present at the king's council and all were straining their wits to find means whereby the king might retain Milan, »draw to him again fugitive Naples»[6], bring all Italy under his jurisdiction, and conquer yet more territories on which he had set his heart. One courtier proposes a league with Venice, another wants to hire German lanceknights, a third the Swiss; others suggest bribing the emperor, bringing over to their side the kings of Aragon and Castile, or concluding peace with England while the Scots must be kept in readiness and a suitable pretender provided lest the English should break away from them and join their enemies.[7] If Hythloday were at that point innocently to suggest that it would be better to leave Italy alone since the kingdom of France is in itself almost too big to be well governed by one man, and if he were to refer to the warning example of the Achorians, »which be situate over against the Island of Utopia on the south-east side»[8], related

above, his advice, as they must all agree, would not be very
well received[1].

Hythloday consequently cannot agree with More's suggestion
in the dialogue that the philosophers should assist their princes
with their counsel for the good of the citizens.[2] They have
not been so unnatural as to withhold it, and many have already
given it in books they have written, but the voice of Socrates
will contend in vain against Thrasymachus and the ideal state
will be impossible to realise, unless kings become indeed philosophers themselves or philosophers attain the royal dignity.[3]
Here once more the author is preparing his readers for the description of his standard example of a well governed community,
Utopia, the country of philosophers, while at the same time he
is attempting yet again to catch the ear of princes by means
of a book on statecraft, but a book, this time, different from
either the *specula principis* to which nobody listened, or the
Moriae Encomium which nobody took seriously, but a book as
exciting as the most sensational tale of travel, cheating them
to listen to »truth thus coated with honey»[4] and making them
swallow the medicine with the sugar. — While in the dialogue
More agrees with the opinion that it is useless to try and force
new and startling views upon minds already made up, he does
not give the battle up for lost. Only the »school philosophy»
(philosophia scholastica) thinks »all things meet for every place».
But there is also a polite philosophy *(philosophia civilior)*, he
says, which is less doctrinaire and knows her place, which does
not fall out of her part by acting a tragic rôle while a comedy
is being performed.[5] Similarly at the courts of princes, if you
cannot wholly remedy abuses confirmed by custom, you must
not utterly forsake the commonwealth any more than you must
abandon the ship in a tempest because you cannot command the
winds. You must speak to people after their own manner, and it
is useless giving advice which cannot be understood. »But you
must with a crafty wile and a subtle train study and endeavour
yourself, as much as in you lies, to handle the matter wittily
and handsomely for the purpose; and that which you cannot
turn to good, so to order it that it be not very bad.»[6]

It is perhaps not entirely beside the point to remember that in his *History of Richard III* More had pointed with approval to the similar behaviour of his former patron, Cardinal Morton, who, while prisoner with the Duke of Buckingham so worked on him as to achieve the union by marriage of the houses of Lancaster and York with the consequent termination of the Wars of the Roses, seeking craftily, i. e. skilfully, »to prick him forward, taking always the occasion of his coming, and so keeping himself close within his bonds that he rather seemed him to follow him than to lead him».[1]

It is important to remember also that More knew well enough that »the whole world is so wretched»[2] that there is nothing perfect in it, and so he goes on speaking in his own person in the dialogue: »For it is not possible for all things to be well, unless all men were good: which I think will not be yet this good many years»[3]. Progress must be slow, and reforms not too radical to be accepted.[4] The point has a bearing on the continuation of this Socratic dialogue, for in Utopia people are not represented as all good. It is not a country like so many modern imitations of it where there is neither crime nor punishment, and so we accept its reality without questioning whether it is at all likely that all men should suddenly become reasonable.

Hythloday, however, can accept no compromise. He does not admit that the reforms which he has suggested, are either »strange or foolishly newfangled». It is not as if he had suggested that all things should be possessed in common, as Plato did or as in fact they are in Utopia That might indeed be as startling as mistaking one's part in a play, since »here amongst us, every man hath his possessions several to himself».[5] Apparently it does not occur even to Raphael that it might be otherwise in Europe. But, being so, it is impossible to improve things substantially even by a »crafty wile and subtle train».[6] As long as there is private property, there will be unequal distribution of wealth[7], and selfishness and greed will seek to acquire ever more riches at the expense of the remainder. This you cannot alter, for if you try and take money from one and give it to another, your »cure of one part» will »make bigger the sore of another part».[8] The evils inherent in our society might well be mitigated but cannot be cured by these means[9], and in this way he tricks us into accepting private property as the root cause of the evils of society and makes us believe in the possibility of »cure».

Now the More of the dialogue objects that if there were no private property there would be no incitement to work and industry.[1] But Raphael assures him that he is wrong, and for proof he tells his story of the Utopians, of their industry and wealth, of their curiosity and anxiousness to increase the sum of their knowledge, and of their work for the improvement of their minds and social conditions. Yet for hundreds of years they have enjoyed complete equality and possessed everything in common. His relation begins with the reference in the first book to the diligence with which they learned everything that some Roman and Alexandrine travellers were able to teach them twelve hundred years ago[2] — another pointed hit at the opponents of humanism — and goes on to the description of their country, their customs and institutions, and, not least, their religion, in the second book. For in humanist fashion the conversation is interrupted for dinner, after which they come out again into the garden and resume their seats upon the same »bench of turves».

I have dwelt so long on this discussion because a German historian of great knowledge, penetration and repute, Professor Hermann Oncken, has maintained that, instead of being, like the stories of the Achorians and the Polylerites, intended as a moral example, the description of the Utopian republic which follows, constitutes More's political ideal, and that *Utopia* must be understood as the programme of a budding politician, expecting his nomination to the cabinet almost at any moment.[3] Renaissance princes certainly prided themselves on adorning their courts with men of learning, and Henry was one of them. More had already been offered a pension by the King, but so far had refused it.[4] To some extent the dialogue does reflect his own problem, but it was not his alone. Pico, whose Life he had translated into English for edification and example, had refused to enter the service of princes with much the same arguments as Hythloday in the dialogue, in a letter translated by More himself.[5] Erasmus, though appointed to the council of Prince Charles, never served in that capacity. It is true that it was not to be granted to Thomas More to pursue his humanist career in complete independence and tranquillity of mind. — He was marked out for martyrdom. — But Erasmus reports that King Henry who »may be said to compel» such men into his service, »could not rest till he had dragged More to court. *Dragged* is the only word; for no aspirant was ever more eager to go to Court than More was to avoid it.»[1] And so, in the phrase of More's contemporary, Vespucci, »inasmuch as the entreaties of Kings are as commands», he yielded to his wishes.[2] More, who always made a virtue of necessity, was then himself to be compelled to use that »crafty wile and subtle train» which he recommends in the dialogue in cases where something cannot be very good, »so to order it that it be not very bad». This, however, does not turn the *Utopia* into a declaration of policy similar to those issued by modern prime ministers on taking office. Still less is there any opportunism in it, as Professor Oncken's amplifying echo Gerhard Ritter suggests.[3] Neither is the identification of Hythloday with More entirely justified. Whoever takes the trouble, or rather does not grudge himself the treat, of reading More's English works and early epigrams, will find that in the dialogue More represents the views that he maintains elsewhere. But to identify Hythloday with Erasmus wholesale, as has been done by another German historian, is going too far by half on the other side.[4] The dialogue is More's version of the contest between the humanist ideal of peace and seclusion in pursuit of knowledge on the one hand and on the other the hard necessity of the world, reflected in his picture of the courts of princes. There are too many parallels in contemporary life and literature to justify us in attributing to it too much of a personal significance.

More's reluctance to tie himself to the King's service made him into one of those few who in Plato's judgment were alone fit to rule[5], but nobody was ever a greater stranger to worldly ambition[6]. The student of literature, consequently, must not shirk the responsibility which is his, to supplement and correct such historians as do not probe the hearts, but are content to observe men only as actors in the political arena and who look upon ideas only as pawns in a game of chess. Speaking of *Utopia* a German scholar has gone the length of maintaining that no notice need be taken of any other work by the same author except the one under discussion, since a book must be interpreted not according to the author's intentions but exclusively according to what it actually says.[1] A book must of course always be its own testimony, but then we must not read things between the lines which are only to be found in the mind of the critic. Our understanding of one book is deepened and not lessened by the study of the rest of an author's work. The historian, who is occupied with the stage of all the world, is not always over-anxious to be just to the individual. He is not always able to muster that deeper sympathy which is required for the understanding of a human being.

But it is time to seek Utopia, situated somewhere in the Western Ocean.

VI

Exactly where Utopia was to be found More was unable to tell as he thought Hythloday had forgotten to mention it and it had not occurred to anybody to ask.[2] When, therefore, a pious divine, thought to have been Rowland Phillips, Vicar of Croydon, desired to go to Utopia as missionary, More could give him no information as to the exact situation of his island and asked Peter Giles to help him.[3] Entering into the spirit of the comedy, Peter Giles answered that he perfectly well remembered Hythloday describing it. Unfortunately exactly at that moment one of More's servants had come up to his master and whispered in his ear, whereas Peter Giles himself had been prevented from hearing because one of the company had been seized with a violent coughing in consequence of a cold caught on ship-board.[4] The Vicar of Croydon consequently had to resign his ambition of becoming the first Bishop of Utopia. Curiously enough he has found not unworthy successors in those German savants who insist on criticizing the Utopians according to the standards applied to the restless nations of Europe.[5] The tribute to More's descriptive power is as flattering as it is unconscious, for these learned men have done nothing but follow in the footsteps of

62739

their master. Machiavelli, whom they praise and hold up as a model of morality, has been accused of some similar naivety in his treatment of mythical and legendary figures, such as Romulus and Remus, Moses and Cyrus, »as if they were all astute politicians of Florentine faction», and not unjustly he has been compared to »the orator in the French Constituent Assembly who proposed to send to Crete for an authentic copy of the Laws of Minos».[1]

Utopia, according to Hythloday, had not always been an island, but was connected with the main land by an isthmus fifteen miles broad. King Utopus, however, from whom the country derived its modern name, had ordered a wide channel to be dug, as broad as the isthmus was long, and so turned Utopia into an island[2], which event was supposed to have taken place one thousand seven hundred and sixty years before Hythloday's visit[3]. King Utopus also had given the island its laws and constitution which had since then remained unaltered. It is notable that by this device More gets round the essential difficulty adhering to all ideal commonwealths, which cannot develop, since if they are perfect, all change must be for the worse. Plato had recourse to all sorts of safeguards to prevent any alteration of the constitution imposed on his Magnesian colony in the *Laws*.[4] More simply assumes that his fictitious commonwealth has existed for nearly two thousand years without other changes than such as were consistent with its democratic constitution. This, however, did not exclude very substantial spiritual and material progress.[5] Hence Victor Rydberg's criticism in the *Vapensmeden* is not entirely justified, although in other respects More would have agreed with him entirely.[6] It is as a fiction Utopia must be criticized, and we must accept More's premises, though not oblivious of the fact that we are up against a witty humanist whose delight it is to confound his readers. Even in the first chapter of the second book More warns us against taking his tale too seriously. »They bring up a great multitude of pullen», he says, »and that by a marvellous policy. For the hens do not sit upon the eggs: but by keeping them in a certain equal heat, they bring life into them, and hatch them. The chickens, as soon as they be come

out of the shell, follow men and women instead of the hens.».[1]
So rational was Utopia that even the animals had been infected
by the general cult of reason, and we can see More smiling at
the wonders he relates, even more marvellous than the most
popular tales of travel.

The background of fact behind Utopia is Vespucci's account
of his travels, first published in the *Cosmographiæ Introductio* by
Waldseemüller at St. Dié in 1507, where the New World, owing to
a misunderstanding, is first named America after Amerigo Vespucci
whose Voyages were appended. This part of the book was frequently reprinted, and More refers to it as »now in print and abroad
in every man's hands».[2] It tells about the natives of the New
World, that they were kind and helpful, usually friendly and on
occasions even generous to foreigners.[3] They despised gold, pearls
and jewelry, and their most coveted treasure consisted in brightly
coloured birds' feathers. They neither sell, he says, nor buy,
nor barter, but are content with what nature freely gives out
of her abundance.[4] They live in perfect liberty and have neither
king nor lord.[5] They observe no laws.[6] They hold their habitations in common, as many as six hundred sharing one building,
and every seven or eight years they move the seat of their
abodes because they fancy the air to have become infected.[7]
They are good swimmers, keep clean, and embrace an Epicurean
philosophy.[8] Those who are aged and going to die they carry
into the forest where they leave them suspended in a net.[9] The
women are skilful with bow and arrows, and when the men go
to war they take the women with them to carry their provisions.
Their wars are vendettas, undertaken if their enemies have captured or killed one of them, never for the increase of territory.[10]
They are unacquainted with the use of iron.[11] There are plenty
of good harbours, and one in particular Vespucci describes as
the finest in the world.[12] All these details from his first voyage
were to return in Utopia after suffering more or less of a sea-
change.

In the small though rapidly expanding world of his day
More cannot have helped being acquainted also with Peter Martyr's work *De orbe novo,* printed in 1511, in which such a rosy
account is given of the West Indies and of the Island of Cuba

in particular. He regards it as proved that there the soil belongs equally to all, like the sun and water. They do not know that difference between mine and thine, which is the cause of all misfortunes. — Hythloday may actually be referring to this account, though not without a side-glance at Plato, in his argument against private property. — It is the Golden Age that they live in. No moats, no walls, no hedges enclose their domains. They live in gardens open to all. Without laws, without constitutions, without judges they act according to nature and the rules of justice. They regard as wicked and criminal all those who take pleasure in hurting their fellow beings.[1] The West Indians, according to Peter Martyr, had an intuitive knowledge of the most essential moral and philosophical truths, and he relates a touching story about an old Guanahani sage who, after attending the Divine service of the Spaniards, instructed Columbus about immortality, informing him concerning the dark and difficult path that after death awaits those who have been tyrants and enemies of mankind, and the alluring road that invites those who have loved peace and the safety of their neighbour. »If», he said, »you are mortal and consider that each soul will receive what she deserves, you will abstain from doing harm to anybody.»[2] Once more a picture that went into the making of Utopia as the very basis of morality and religion in More's imaginary commonwealth. There is no need to assume that More was in possession of any occult knowledge of the Incas of Peru, not to be discovered until many years after the publication of *Utopia*. What likeness there exists between these two is confined to such general traits as are common to the West Indian and South American civilizations before the coming of the Inca conquerors.

Professor Yrjö Hirn has suggested that the Renaissance idea of the Golden Age had mingled in the minds of men with the myth of an earthly paradise in the mediæval tales of travel, so that with joint forces these conceptions coloured the descriptions of the New World.[3] Perhaps a lingering memory of the lost Atlantis in Plato's *Critias* and *Timaeus* was also playing in the imagination of the travellers. However that may be, for his description of the new island of Utopia More could draw on facts well known to his contemporaries and taken for granted by the reading public. His subsidiary sources were ancient Greek or Roman. In the *Germania* of Tacitus he found a picture much to his purpose. Details were fetched out of other classical authors, such as Aristotle and Plutarch, Cicero, Caesar, and Pliny.[1] But Erasmus tells us that as a young man More had in a dialogue defended the communism of Plato, including the community of women.[2] Hence it is no matter for surprise that the natives of the Western archipelago who lived according to the law of nature, should have captured his imagination.

VII

Unlike Plato More does not confine communism to the ruling classes. In Utopia there are no classes, if by class we mean the hereditary privileges or disabilities which separated the citizens in Plato's *Republic* and caused them to be referred to one or another of four distinct groups of society. In Utopia there is neither private property nor hereditary privilege. The social distinctions that there are to be found, are entirely based on merit. Criminals are condemned to servitude, whereas citizens who particularly distinguish themselves in intellectual pursuits can be excused from manual labour.[3] But just as the serf can regain his status of a free citizen by diligence and genuine repentance[4], so the learned are mercilessly degraded if they do not come up to expectation[5]. Everybody is born free and given the same opportunities. The same education is provided for all, women as well as men[6], and all are expected to do the same amount of work[7]. No idleness is tolerated, and thanks to the fact that everybody performs manual labour, the hours of work can be restricted to six a day or even less.[8] Yet in the absence of the vast group of idlers to be found in European states, sufficient and more than sufficient is produced for everybody.[9] In Utopia only five hundred out of an adult population of between 60 000 and 100 000 in each city are excused from manual labour, and the two hundred Phylarchs who are among those exempt by statute, volunteer for work in order to give an example to the rest and encourage them to work all the better. Consequently only three hundred citizens devote themselves exclusively to learned studies. They are all the more respected, and out of this small number the higher magistrates are elected.[1]

Agriculture is the chief industry and an occupation which all the citizens must learn. Hence they are made to spend two years in the country, being at liberty to remain there if they choose. In this way, and by means of an annual exchange of half the country population, a constant circulation is kept up between town and country.[2] Sufficient labour is always available, and the balance between agriculture and other industries is preserved. The result is that there is never any shortage of food, and when necessary the harvest can be gathered almost in a day, given favourable weather; for, unlike the conditions in some other ideal commonwealths, the Utopian climate is not excessively good, nor the soil very fertile.[3] Out of the surplus produced, a reserve is laid up sufficient to meet two years' consumption in case of famine. And even after that has been done there is enough agricultural produce left over to enable the Utopians to maintain a flourishing export trade.[4]

Otherwise they are at liberty to choose their own occupations, although by preference they devote themselves to their fathers' craft. The women work in such occupations as best fit their constitutions, e. g. the making of cloth from flax or wool, whereas the men become masons, blacksmiths, and carpenters.[5] Particularly heavy labour, or such menial occupations as the Utopians are reluctant to perform, is either voluntarily done by members of a religious sect, who believe that hard toil in this world will gain them felicity in the next[6], or else by serfs or bondmen. The latter are of various kinds. One category consists of Utopians convicted of some grievous offence and so condemned to hard labour. Others are men condemned to death in other countries but saved by the Utopians who buy them for a mere pittance and so preserve their lives. A third category consists of people who prefer servitude in Utopia to poverty and want in another country. The last mentioned are treated almost like free citizens, except that they are made to do a little more work because they are used to it. Their own criminals receive the harshest treatment, since having been brought up to virtue in the best of commonwealths they can offer no excuse for their misdeeds. Magistrates are more severely punished than ordinary citizens.[1]

Even so Utopia does not become the slave state for which it has been mistaken by German critics[2], for good behaviour is rewarded with release from bondage, and relapse into crime is punished by death. Thus the proportion of bondmen to free citizens is no more than five per cent, which is hardly excessive, considering that a number of grave offences are punished with penal servitude, as we would term the Utopian bondage.[3] It is just that instead of hanging their thieves, the Utopians put them to work, this method being »to the commonwealth more profitable». The presence of foreign serfs, moreover, is intended to show that bondage is not such a hard lot after all, since servitude in Utopia is preferable to freedom elsewhere. A comparison with ancient Rome or Athens would not be unfavourable to Utopia.

All citizens dress alike in coarse garments of white linen and cloaks of natural wool.[4] Only the prince is distinguished by the sheaf of corn that is carried in front of him, and the head of the church is similarly distinguished by a wax taper.[5] All vanities are held in the utmost contempt.[6] The houses are all similar, but so solidly built that no time is unnecessarily wasted in repairs or new construction, and every ten years they exchange houses, just as the West Indians in Vespucci's Voyages moved their habitations every seven or eight years. There is no lock to the doors and so no privacy.[7] They have nothing to conceal and nothing to guard. But behind the houses are those gardens of which Peter Martyr had spoken and in which the Utopians take exceedingly great pleasure. There they spend much of their time labouring to make them beautiful and in summer enjoying there the cool of the evening. Street even competes with street as to which is possessed of the better row of gardens.[8]

For the rest they employ their leisure in study. Lectures are provided for those selected for learning, but many others avail themselves of this opportunity of improving their minds. This they may easily do since »in the institution of that weal public this end is only and chiefly pretended and minded, that what time may possibly be spared from the necessary occupations and affairs of the commonwealth, all that the citizens should withdraw from the bodily service to the free liberty of the mind and garnishing of the same».[1] They are eminent musicians, take a deep interest in natural philosophy, arithmetic, geometry, and astronomy, but astrology they hold in contempt.[2] In philosophy they equal the ancient Greeks, but they have no sense of the importance of the distinctions of the *Parva Logicalia*. »They reason of virtue and Pleasure. But the chief and principal question is in what thing, be it one or more, the felicity of man consisteth.»[3]

They despise gold, and lest a taste for it should develop, they do not lock it up, but put it to the most hateful and contemptible uses. The most hardened criminals are fettered in chains of gold, gold rings and necklaces are the marks of less dangerous convicts, and so gold with them has become a sign of infamy. Of pearls and precious stones, which, as Vespucci had reported, were not valued by the natives of the West Indies any more than gold or silver, they make toys and trinkets for their children, who naturally throw them away as they grow up.[4] These habits necessarily lead to amusing misunderstandings when strangers unacquainted with their habits visit Utopia. This happens when ambassadors arrive from the Anemolians (»windbags»), decked with gold and precious stones, according to the custom of the time. We can see them looking, in More's phrase, »like devils out of hell»[5], and the children of Amaurote (»the city of shadows»), capital of Utopia, who have already thrown away their toys, dig their mothers between the ribs and point at the head of the embassy and ask who that great idiot may be who walks about covered with trinkets as if he were still a child. »Peace, son», comes the answer, »I think he be some of the ambassadors' fools.» But before they leave Utopia, even the Anemolian ambassadors have doffed their gorgeous trimmings and learned that it is foolish for a man to take pleasure »in the glistering of a little trifling stone, who may behold any of the stars or else the sun itself».[6] Thus Raphael Hythloday's relation of his adventures is not free from moralizing reflections to which the reader will do well to pay attention if he wants to understand More's meaning. Altogether his tale achieves much livelier effects in its rambling inconsistencies than any account of it can hope to attempt.

Plato had abolished the family among the governing classes and introduced strictly regulated sex relations in its stead, in order to ensure the best possible hereditary conditions, but More follows St. Augustine, about whose *City of God* he had as a young man lectured in Grocyn's church of St. Lawrence Jewry[1], and makes the family the very basis of society. Vespucci had related that the West Indians were entirely promiscuous[2], and such scrupulous regard does More evince for the verisimilitude of his story, that he goes out of his way to make the Utopians an exception, meticulously underlining that »they only of the nations in that part of the world be content every man with one wife apiece»[3]. Measures are taken to ensure that marriages shall be both congenial and physically sound. Before the marriage ceremony »a sad and honest matron showeth the woman, be she maid or widow, naked to the wooer. And likewise a sage and discreet man exhibiteth the wooer naked to the woman.» We may laugh at this as foolish, says Raphael,

> »but they on the other part do greatly wonder at the folly of all other nations, which in buying a colt, where as a little money is in hazard, be so chary and circumspect, that though he be almost all bare, yet they will not buy him, unless the saddle and all the harness be taken off, lest under those coverings be hid some gall or sore; and yet in choosing a wife, which shall be either pleasure or displeasure to them all their life after, they be so reckless, that, all the residue of the woman's body being covered with clothes, they esteem her scarcely by one hand-breadth (for they can see no more but her face); and so do join her to them not without great jeopardy of evil agreeing together, if anything in her body afterwards do offend and mislike them».[4]

— This custom, which is hardly to be taken literally, contrasts sharply with the child marriages then customary among the royal and noble families of Europe, yet I doubt whether More had anything else in mind except the gravity of a decision that affects the whole of a man's or woman's after-life.[5]

Once the marriage is accomplished, it is difficult to dissolve. This is done in cases of adultery when the offenders are condemned to the »most grievous bondage». The other parties whose marriages have thus been broken without any fault of their own, may marry each other, if they want to, or they may follow their former companions into bondage, in which case it often happens that the repentance of the one and the earnest endeavours of the other move the prince's pity so that he restores the culprit to freedom. Otherwise the innocent party is allowed to marry again, a privilege refused to adulterers. Such as have had sexual intercourse without wedlock are debarred from marriage altogether. Repeated adultery is punished with death.[1] A divorce can be granted by the Council on account of »intolerable wayward manners of either party», in which case the one who is innocent of any offence, is allowed to marry again; or else, if the man and woman cannot agree together, but both have a good chance of happiness in a new marriage. There are no other recognized grounds for divorce, and even in these instances the Council is »loth to consent to it, because they know this to be the next way to break love between man and wife, to be in easy hope of a new marriage».[2] — Again this sanctity of the marriage tie is no doubt intended as a contrast to the loose morals and the »connubial facility of the age».[3]

The husband chastizes his wife, and the parents their children, and the younger always wait upon the elder.[4] Special care is taken of the sick and aged. As in London before the confiscations of King Henry four magnificent hospitals provide cure for the sick who are there tended by »cunning physicians».[5] But if anybody is incurably ill and suffering grievous pain without hope of relief, he may, with the sanction of the priest and magistrates, if he wants to be rid of his pain and die, either »dispatch himself out of that painful life» or have it done by others. Without these provisions, however, suicide is strongly disapproved of, and the body »as unworthy both of the earth and of fire, they cast unburied into some stinking marsh».[6] — We may suppose this practice of euthanasia to have been inspired by Vespucci's Voyages, and More would have adopted it the more readily since it seemed to be in agreement with the doctrine of the ancient Stoics.

The sons do not leave their homes on getting married, but bring their wives there, and as the children grow up the sons in their turn will bring young wives home, until the households under the patriarchal rule of the eldest male member must resemble More's own house at Chelsea, where, however, the daughters also remained with their husbands.[1] The number of adult members of the Utopian households is limited to sixteen, and lest it should be exceeded children are if necessary transferred to less numerous families, so that a minimum of ten adults is always maintained. The households are bigger in the country, where they consist of forty adult members and two bondmen. If a city should threaten to become overpopulated, a migration of citizens to a less populous city is arranged, so that, the number of households remaining constant, the population of the island is kept between the limits indicated by the statutory size of the families. The exact number of citizens, on the other hand, is not fixed, as in Plato's *Republic* and *Laws*, and there is no need to put out superfluous children as in the *Republic*. If an overpopulation of the whole island should occur and the means of livelihood be endangered, then recourse is had to the device of the *Laws* and a colony sent forth »in friendly wise».[2] A certain number of citizens are then selected from the fifty-four cities in the island to build a new town on the neighbouring continent where there is »much waste and unoccupied ground». What inhabitants there are, are offered the option of living as free citizens under the laws of Utopia. If they are wicked enough to refuse, they are expelled, and should they »resist and rebel», it means war, for the Utopians regard »this as the most just cause of war, when any people holdeth a piece of ground void and vacant to no good nor profitable use, keeping others from the use and possession of it, which notwithstanding by the law of nature ought thereof to be nourished and relieved». Should, however, the population of the Island of Utopia fall under the statutory limit, the colonists return in sufficient numbers to make up the deficit, and colonial towns may in this manner »decay and perish».[3] — The contrast is notable between the classical motives that inspired the behaviour of the Utopians, and the recommendations given in Machiavelli's *Principe,* already finished in manuscript in Tuscany though not printed until many years later. To the latter the sole motive was the subjection of a conquered people, and the best means to achieve it was to found colonies in a few places to serve as keys to the new dominion.[1]

The streets of Amaurote — and all the cities are alike — are broad and the houses well and solidly built of stone. The hygienic arrangements are perfect.[2] Indeed, nothing could present a greater contrast to those overcrowded, dark, smelly nests of disease and pestilence which in Europe bore the flattering name of towns and cities. The Utopian towns are all bright, airy, and healthy. They are divided into four quarters, and each quarter into fifty local units. Thirty families form one such »ward» which possesses a great hall where they have their meals in common, the women on one side of the table, the men on the other, and not as in Plato's *Laws* in separate messes. Mothers with small children, however, eat in a special nursery. Not that it is forbidden to take food home from the markets of which there is one in each quarter, but the Utopians think »it were a folly to take the pain to dress a bad dinner at home, when they may be welcome to good and fine fare so nigh hand at the hall».[3] Along the table old and young alternate, so that the latter may learn a courteous behaviour and profit by the conversation of their elders. Each meal begins with a short lesson which provides subjects for a profitable conversation, which is by no means monopolized by the old who, on the contrary, encourage the young also to say their say.[4]

The thirty households of each ward annually elect an officer called Syphogrant or, with a name derived from Plato, Phylarch, who presides in Hall and is the magistrate and representative of the ward. Ten syphogrants with their three hundred households between them annually elect a Tranibor or Chief Phylarch, who is usually re-elected unless he should be guilty of some offence. The Prince or, more properly, Mayor, is elected by the two hundred syphogrants among four candidates chosen by the people, one from each quarter of the city. He is the only Utopian magistrate who holds his office for life. Yet this arrangement can hardly have been modelled on the Tudor monarchy, as Professor Hertzler thinks.[1] His intimate knowledge of party strife and parliamentary misrule in fifteenth century England would have taught More the value of continuity and authority, represented by the Utopian *princeps*. Yet even the prince only holds his office for life, »unless he be deposed or put down for suspicion of tyranny». For it is a notable feature of Utopian justice that the mere intention counts as equally punishable with the crime.[2] Hence the Utopian order must rather be interpreted as a protest against the Tudor tyranny, as instituted by Henry VII, and it is not amiss to remember that other European countries enjoyed even less constitutional freedom than the England of the Tudors.

The Utopian prince can reach no decisions in affairs of state, unless supported by the council of tranibors. Each of the twenty tranibors further summons two syphogrants to aid him, so that the Council comes to consist of sixty magistrates, presided over by the Prince. The syphogrants serve only one day in turn, so that at every new sitting two thirds of the members are new. No important matter can be decided until it has been under debate for three days. Consequently no fewer than one hundred and twenty syphogrants will have had an opportunity of making their views known. The syphogrants further debate the matter with all the families in their wards. Specially important decisions are referred to the council of the whole island, to which each of the fifty-four cities sends three representatives. On no question whatsoever can decision be taken the day it is introduced, the discussion of it being deferred to the next sitting.[3] By their constitution the Utopians are thus ensured the right of themselves choosing their rulers, and are guaranteed the control of their activities. On the other hand, it is forbidden to debate matters of state outside the council chamber, lest the Prince and tranibors should conspire against the state and bring about an alteration of the constitution. Offences against this law are punished with death.[4]

Not the least important duty of the magistrates is the education of the people, for although only a limited number are priviliged to pursue learning as a career, education belongs to all and to men and women equally. It is in this way that Utopia becomes a state of philosophers, an achievement indeed for a democracy which offers the same opportunities to all. Even so Utopia would hardly have become the ideal of so many social reformers, if it had not been for the public spirit that informs her citizens. Laws are few — an ideal visualized by Plato and dreamed of also by Erasmus and Vives as well as Bellamy.[1] But the magistrates are like fathers to the people, just as Cicero, Pliny, and Erasmus held that they should be.[2] Altogether that state of complete confidence and collaboration seems to be realised in Utopia, which St. Augustine had described in his *City of God*, where even those who rule actually serve those whom they seem to govern.[3] In Utopia all efforts are directed towards the common good, and since nobody possesses anything as his own, every citizen works for the welfare of all.

Epicureans though More made them, in reliance on Vespucci, they yet prefer the pleasures of the mind to those of the body. The greatest pleasure of all is the consciousness of a good deed.[4] For while nature prescribes a joyful life, »verily she commands thee» not to seek it at any one else's expense, but on the contrary to do everything to help others to it. And so, since pleasure taken in virtue outweighs all others, More, by means of a clever device, gets his Utopians to seek virtue for the pleasure it brings.[5] Indeed, no pleasure need be forbidden as long as it causes no harm.[6] And so tender are their consciences that they will by no means approve of hunting which they regard as »the lowest, vilest, and most abject part of butchery». And lest their minds should be inured to cruelty the Utopians do not exercise the craft of butchery, to which only bondmen are appointed.[7] But to keep faith with men and observe the public laws, this they consider to be such stuff as pleasure is made on.[8] And since the laws are made for their mutual advantage, they do not feel the severity of the law as a painful compulsion, but gain their freedom within the law by identifying their own individual will with the common good.

VIII

In economic matters the whole island is like one family, the surplus of one city being freely given to another. In accordance with the hints given by Vespucci, however, there is one commodity they entirely lack, namely iron, which on account of its usefulness they prize far above gold and silver. In order to be able to import it, they sell abroad the surplus products of their own industries, such as grain, wood, wool and flax, furs and leather, cattle, honey, wax, tallow and dies, in quantities far in excess of the needs of their own imports. The charitable disposition, characteristic of their internal trade, marks also their commercial relations with foreign countries. Not only do they always sell at a reasonable price, but one seventh part of all the goods exported they freely give to the poor of the other nation. They can import all the iron they need, and for the rest they do not care whether they are paid in ready money. They are just as pleased that the money should be used by the foreign state which needs it better, and they only claim it in case of war or if they have to lend it to another country. »The most part of it they never ask. For that thing which is to them no profit, to take it from others to whom it is profitable, they think it no right nor conscience.»[1] In More's mind there is no suspicion of any commercial exploitation or imperialistic aspirations. These exist only in the minds of his German critics.[2]

However, the production of the busy Utopians is so great that in spite of their generosity they accumulate vast treasures of gold and silver at home also. Since they have no use for them, they keep them solely for the uncertain event of war, »which as it may happen, so it may be that it shall never come to pass».

In speaking of Utopian warfare More's irony reaches triumphant heights. Raphael Hythloday is made to hesitate whether he dare mention it at all, for fear lest his »words shall not be believed. And this I have more cause to fear, for that I know how difficultly and hardly I myself would have believed another man telling the same, if I had not presently seen it with mine own eyes. For it must needs be, that how far a thing is dissonant and disagreeing from the guise and trade of the hearers, so far shall it be out of their belief.» And thus he brazenly labels an account which is no more than a slight caricature of the common European practice. The Utopians know, we are told, »that for money enough their enemies themselves many times may be bought and sold, or else through treason be set together by the ears among themselves». And since they had rather »put strangers in jeopardy than their own countrymen», they put their money aside »especially and chiefly to hire therewith, and that for unreasonable great wages, strange soldiers».[1] — The only difference between Utopia and Europe is that whereas the Utopians had reserved money for the purpose, European princes had to extort it from the taxpayer or the mercenaries had it out of the people whose country they happened to occupy, be it friend or foe. But More's manner has puzzled many of his critics and annoyed some.[2] Yet it is a mode of expression which he uses more than once exactly as a channel for his most bitter irony. — »This custom of buying and selling adversaries», i. e. to serve as traitors and assassins, he says, »among other peoples is disallowed, as a cruel act of a base and a cowardish mind». For it is notable that More lets no opportunity slip of pouring scorn also on the empty show of chivalry, which still survived the passing of its virtues.

»But they in this behalf think themselves much praiseworthy, as who like wise men by this means dispatch great wars without any battle or skirmish. Yea, they count it also a deed of pity and mercy, because that by the death of a few offenders the lives of a great number of innocents, as well of their own men as also of their enemies, be ransomed and saved, which in fighting should have been slayn. For they do no less pity the base and common sort of their enemy's people, than they do their own; knowing that they be driven to war against their wills by the furious madness of their princes and heads.»[3]

But the Utopians do not go to war lightly, for »war and battle as a thing very beastly, . . . they do detest and abhor, and contrary to the custom almost of all other nations, they count nothing so much against glory, as glory gotten in war».[1] Within the Island of Utopia »none of the cities desire to enlarge the bounds and limits of their shires».[2] This is quite natural to them, because they refuse to recognize two distinct codes of law, one applying to the private citizen and the other to states and the heads of states,

>one ... going afoot and creeping by low on the ground, and bound down on every side with many bands, because it shall not run at rovers: the other a princely virtue, which, like as it is of much higher majesty than the other poor justice, so also it is of much more liberty, as to the which nothing is unlawful that it lusteth after».

— One would believe these words to have been written as a comment to *The Prince*, so straight is the aim at the Machiavellian politics of European monarchs. — In Utopia, however, the same law that governs the relations of individuals, governs also international relations.[3] It is entirely based on mutual confidence and the ties of natural friendship. These they refuse to replace by leagues artificially made, chiefly because »in those parts of the world leagues between princes be wont to be kept and observed very slenderly». They might change their minds, More ironically suggests, if they saw how religiously such agreements are kept in Europe »partly through the justice and goodness of princes, and partly through the reverence of popes».[4] — One need not be an historian to see whom More is aiming at. Had not his confessor John Colet admonished his prince, with an obvious play on the names of two warlike popes, »not to follow the ⌐ample of Julius and Alexander»?[5] — The Utopians, however, disapprove of leagues even on principle. If alliances were necessary, they argue, people must believe that they were born enemies and that unless they were in league it would be right to try and exterminate each other. They might even start searching for loop-holes in the treaty in order to find an excuse for attacking each other. The Utopians, on the contrary, regard the bonds of nature as a link between nations strong enough to overcome the little hills and rivers which separate them, and think »that no man ought to be counted an enemy, which hath done no injury; and that the fellowship of nature is a strong league; and that men be better and more surely knit together by love and benevolence, than by covenants of leagues; by hearty affection of mind, than by words».[1]

But lest »the envy of foreign princes»[2] should place their state in jeopardy, the Utopians have reinforced their natural island fortress with such strong defences »that a few defenders may drive back many armies»[3]. Nor do they neglect physical training. They even breed fierce horses for the training of their young men in the art of riding, while using oxen as draught animals because they are hardier and possess the additional advantage of being edible after their work is done. The whole nation, men and women alike, as in Plato, are trained in the use of arms and the discipline of war, so as not to be found wanting if the need should arise.[4]

If anybody should disturb the international order and break against the laws governing international relations, the Utopians go to war

»in the defence of their own country, or to drive out of their friends' lands the enemies that be comen in, or by their power to deliver from the yoke and bondage of tyranny some people that be oppressed with tyranny. Which thing they do of mere pity and compassion.»

Provided they are consulted beforehand, they may even go to the assistance of their friends in order to revenge an injury for which compensation is refused by the aggressors. And this they do, not only if the territory of their friends is invaded, but also if the merchants of that country should suffer wrong or receive unjust treatment under the pretext of inequitable laws.[5] — More has made it abundantly clear that there is no question of any imperialistic policy. The sole reasons for war that the Utopians acknowledge are defensive, be it in defence of their own country and that of other victims of aggression or of the rights of free citizens of their own or other countries against indigenous or foreign oppressors. The casuistry of which More has been accused by acrimonious critics is entirely of their own making. In addition it is notable that the Utopians do not resort to war where their own money is in the balance, since they can afford to lose it, and can content themselves with interrupting all trade relations with such as do not keep contracts; but they pursue with ferocity the quarrels of their friends whose money is in private hands, if trial prove them just. Their battle is for the preservation of justice and peace in the defence of that international order which alone makes commerce possible between nations. It is wholly consistent with the strict rule of law in Utopia itself, and just as offences against it by private individuals are severely punished, so the same code is applied to the relations between states and nations. The wars in which the Utopians reluctantly indulge are nothing but the application of those sanctions without which no law can continue being held in respect.[1] Where criminals go unpunished a state of anarchy results, be it in matters under national or international jurisdiction, before civil courts or the courts of nations. The question is of some importance, for at a time when Christendom under its two heads, the Emperor and Pope, was being split into national states and churches, More suffered martyrdom in the cause of international law, set at naught by his murderers.[2]

If the Utopians do go to war, their manner of pursuing it is such as to warn all instigators not to provoke them a second time.[3] Bloodshed, however, they avoid as far as possible, »counting it a great folly to buy precious wares too dear», and we are reminded of Colet's and Erasmus' argument that the cost of war is in every case so great as under no circumstances ever to justify it, and that an unjust peace is preferable to a just war. »With bodily strength (say they) bears, lions, bores, wolves, dogs, and other wild beasts do fight», but only men can conquer »by the might and puissance of wit». And consequently »they rejoice and avaunt themselves, if they vanquish and oppress their enemies by craft and deceit. And for that act they make a general triumph.»[4] Immediately war is declared, they plaster the enemy cities with proclamations in which »they promise great rewards to him that will kill their enemy's prince» and other of their leaders, but if they should be captured and brought to the Utopians alive, they double the rewards. These promises the Utopians never break. Yet, if this means should prove insufficient,

»they procure occasions of debate and dissention to be spread among their enemies, as by bringing the prince's brother, or some of the noblemen, in hope to obtain the kingdom. If this way prevail not, then they raise up the people that be next neighbours and borderers to their enemies, and them they set in their necks under the colour of some old title of right, such as kings do never lack. To them they promise their help and aid in their war. And as for moneys they give them abundance; but of their own citizens they send to them few or none.»[1]

The description is obviously ironical and such a tangible parody of contemporary European warfare that it seems well-nigh incredible that it should ever have been misunderstood.[2]

It is true that in order to give food for thought, More attributes to the Utopians a greater love of their own citizens than can be laid to the charge of any contemporary European monarch, but his description of the zapoletes (»those who are ready to sell themselves») only drives home his vigorous argument against mercenaries in the first book.[3]

»They be hideous, savage, and fierce, dwelling in wild woods and high mountains, where they were bred and brought up. They be of an hard nature, able to abide and sustain heat, cold, and labour; abhorring from all delicate dainties, occupying no husbandry nor tillage of the ground, homely and rude both in the building of their houses and in their apparel; given unto no goodness, but only to the breed and bringing up of cattle. The most part of their living is by hunting and stealing. They be born only to war, which they diligently and earnestly seek for. And when they have gotten it, they be wonders glad thereof. They go forth of their country in great companies together, and whosoever lacketh soldiers, there they proffer their service for small wages. This is the only craft that they have to get their living by. They maintain their life by seeking their death. For them, whomwith they be in wages, they fight hardly, fiercely, and faithfully. But they bind themselves for no certain time. But upon this condition they enter into bonds, that the next day they will take part with the other side for greater wages; and the next day after that they will be ready to come back again for a little more money. There be few wars there away, wherein is not a great number of them in both parties. Therefore it daily chanceth that nigh kinsfolk, which were hired together on one part, and there very friendly and familiarly used themselves one with another, shortly after, being separate into contrary parts, run one against another enviously and fiercely; and forgetting both kindred and friendship, thrust their swords one in another: and that for none other cause, but that they be hired of contrary princes for a little money. Which they do so highly regard and esteem, that they will easily be provoked to change parts for a halfpenny more wages by the day. So quickly they have taken a smack in covetousness; which for all that is to them no profit. For, that they get by fighting, immediately they spend unthriftily and wretchedly in riot.»¹

More's detestation is obvious. This is no part of his ideal. But it is exactly what was happening in Europe even at the very moment he was writing, and the worst was yet to come. — The Utopians use the Zapoletes with the cynicism they deserve, seeing that war is fit for none other than beasts.

»This people fight for the Utopians against all nations, because they give them greater wages, than any other nation will. For the Utopians, like as they seek good men to use well, so they seek these evil and vicious men to abuse. Whom, when need requireth, with promises of great rewards they put forth into great jeopardies; from whence the most part of them never cometh again to ask their rewards. But to them that remain on live they pay that which they promised faithfully, that they may be the more willing to put themselves in like dangers another time. Nor the Utopians pass not how many of them they bring to destruction. For they believe that they should do a very good deed for all mankind, if they could rid out of the world all that foul, stinking den of that most wicked and cursed people.»²

Remembering that More regarded the mercenaries as one of the causes of war and one of the curses of peace in Europe, it is not difficult to see that he did not want to give any encouragement to such an institution. The reminder that it is irreconcilable with human dignity and the respect due to the value of the individual was one of the lessons most necessary to the times in which he lived.

The Utopians help their friends with money and mercenaries, and encourage other friends to help them. But on the whole they require them to look after the defence of their own soil themselves, just as the Utopians never use foreign troops in their own island. Only when it becomes necessary do they support others with their own armed forces.³ Only volunteers are used in foreign expeditions, and nobody is made to fight abroad against his will, lest he should prove a bad soldier. If the war should be carried into their own country, on the other hand, they conscript everybody, and then they turn even the faint-hearted into good and useful soldiers by interspersing some among the crews manning their ships of war and others among the garrisons of forts from where they cannot flee, and they have found that extreme necessity may often turn a coward into a hero.[1]

Vespucci had related that in the West Indies the women accompanied the men on warlike expeditions, and More was always particularly pleased when he could find a parallel in Plato and so establish a wider basis for the reasonable behaviour of his Utopians. In the *Republic* women go to war with the men, and even the children are brought to watch the battles from a distance as apprentices. With the community of women which is established, there are of course no families, except in so far as the whole guardian class forms a kind of large family whose members address all others as brothers, fathers, or sons, depending on their age. For this reason, says Plato, they would be least likely to desert each other and so most successful in war. And if the women were to join in their campaigns, either in the ranks or marshalled behind to intimidate the enemy by the increase of their numbers, that, in his view, would make them irresistible.[2] The Utopian women are therefore not only allowed to volunteer, but even encouraged to do so.

»And in set field the wives do stand every one by her own husband's side. Also every man is compassed next about with his own children, kinsfolk, and alliance; that they, whom nature chiefly moveth to mutual succour, thus standing together, may help one another. It is a great reproach and dishonesty for the husband to come home without his wife, or the wife without her husband, or the son without his father.»[3]

The contrast with European practice, as caricatured in the behaviour of the Zapoletes, could not be more emphatic.

Although they try every possible means not to become involved in war, if justice requires it the Utopians do fight, and then their courage and skill in battle equal their wisdom in keeping out of it as long as possible. If their adversaries are equally determined and so force a bloody decision, the battle is fought with such ferocity that it may end in the »utter destruction of both parties». Picked battalions of Utopians usually break through the enemy lines and secure their captain, dead or alive. They are equally expert at laying and avoiding an ambush, at outmanoeuvering their enemies and preserving their own lines intact. Like the West Indians they are expert swimmers, and they have all learned to swim in harness. They are ingenious in the construction of field fortifications and the invention of engines of war, and there is never any leakage of information concerning their »secret weapons».[1]

On the other hand, the Utopians keep truce religiously, even under severe provocation. They do not slaughter fleeing enemies but even try and save them from being trodden down by men and horses, »thinking», says More with an eye to Europe, »that it groweth for their own use and profit». They hurt no one who is unarmed, unless he is a spy. They do not ravage and lay waste their enemy's country, as was always done in Europe. They do not sack the cities and kill the inhabitants, except the leaders, who are executed, and the soldiers, who are put to servitude. They take no spoil, but they reward those who have helped them. Nor do they ask their friends to contribute to the cost of the war, all of which is charged to their defeated enemies. Part of the indemnities they receive in ready money and keep in reserve for the eventuality of another war, another part they prefer to receive in annual revenues to be collected by an officer who resides in that country and »lives there sumptuously». Often, however, they lend this money to their former enemies and in that case they seldom ask to have it back.[2]

This is the manner in which More has developed the theme of what Vespucci called a war of »vendetta» and what we would call a war »to end wars». It was intended no doubt as a writing on the wall, addressed to the warlike princes of Europe whom More held alone responsible for the wars devastating the continent at the time when he wrote. It tended to be all the more effective since the Utopians, faithful to their view that the mere intention should be equally punishable with the crime, »if any prince stir up war against them, intending to invade their land, they meet him incontinent out of their own borders with great power and strength».[1] Utopian warfare is in itself an argument against war.

War with the Utopians, however, is a painful exception, and in their island fortress they can look with reasonable confidence to a peaceful future. Curiously enough it is not impossible that the *Utopia* may have had some contemporary influence in this respect, for Henry VIII became a great gunnery expert and started fortifying the coasts of England. We are so used to regarding an island as relatively secure against invasion that we forget this was not always so. In the days of slow and laborious land communications an island empire was more vulnerable than any other state, for an enemy fleet, as Sir John Fortescue pointed out, could strike at any part of it before the defences could be prepared, and it was more difficult for friends and allies to come to its rescue since an auxiliary force required a fleet to command the seas in order safely to transport the troops, and a fleet was neither built nor equipped in a day.[2] The point is apposite because More's German antagonists have founded their identification of Utopian warfare with British imperialism on the false supposition of England's impregnable situation and security against attack from the continent of Europe.[3] Yet invading armies ought to be no news to readers of the Histories of Shakespeare.

Utopian security does not rest on fortifications and preparedness alone. Their relations with foreign countries are founded on mutual trust. And so strong is the confidence, so great the admiration of Utopian justice, that »their next neighbours and borderers, which live free and under no subjection», send to Utopia for magistrates,

»some for a year, and some for five years' space. Which, when the time of their office is expired, they bring home again with honour and praise; and take new ones again with them into their country. These nations have undoubtedly very well and wholesomely provided for their commonwealths. For seeing that both the making and the marring of the weal public doth depend and hang on the manners of the rulers and magistrates, what officers could they more wisely have chosen, than those which cannot be led from honesty by bribes (for to them that shortly after shall depart thence into their own country

money should be unprofitable); nor yet be moved either with favour
or malice towards any man, as being strangers and unacquainted
with the people? The which two vices of affection and avarice
where they take place in judgments, incontinent they break justice,
the strongest and surest bond of a commonwealth. These peoples,
which fetch their officers and rulers from them, the Utopians call
their fellows; and others, to whom they have been beneficial, they
call their friends.»¹

It is a far cry from this picture of »worthy and uncorrupt
magistrates»² to the programme of capitalist exploitation which
More's detractors have been anxious to father upon him³.

IX

Their elevated morals the Utopians derive from their religion.
It is a natural religion, entirely founded on reason, and yet it
is in some respects more spiritualized than many a doctrine
then preached throughout Europe. The Utopians worship God
under different forms. Some worship the sun, others the moon,
others again one of the planets. A few worship as their god,
and highest of all gods, a man whose virtue was greater than
that of all others. But the majority, and among these the wisest
among them, believe in »a certain godly power unknown, ever-
lasting, incomprehensible, inexplicable, far above the capacity
and reach of man's wit, dispersed throughout all the world, not
in bigness, but in virtue and power. Him they call the father
of all. To him alone they attribute the beginnings, the increas-
ings, the proceedings, the changes, and the ends of all things.
Neither they give divine honours to any others than to him.»⁴

Actually all agree that there is one principal god who has
created and governs the universe, although they cannot agree
about his nature. Yet that doctrine which is embraced by the
wisest of them, has gained ever more adherents and would not
have failed being universally adopted, if for superstitious reasons
converts had not attributed their little personal mishaps to the
revengeful spirit of that god whose worship they were about to
desert. — In this manner one is reminded of the fact that they
had no St. Augustine to set them right. — Christianity also
has gained many adherents among them, principally because the

fact that Jesus Christ had possessed everything in common with his disciples appealed to them.[1]

All sects are allowed freely to exercise their religions, since the Utopians have no means of deciding which is true, and the founder of their commonwealth, King Utopus, believed that diversity of worship might not be displeasing to God. He was further convinced that if there is one true doctrine, while all others are vain superstitions, then truth of its own inherent power must finally be victorious, provided only that the matter is settled reasonably and without violence. Hence it is permitted openly to discuss religious questions and even to try and convert others by argument, but it is forbidden to use threats or violence.[2]

The religious toleration of the Utopians, however, is not unlimited. Those who think that the world is governed by chance without any divine providence and so deny the existence of God, or who »conceive so vile and base an opinion of the dignity of man's nature» as to deny the immortality of the soul, are refused the rights of citizenship. Further punishment they need not undergo as long as they keep their belief to themselves. But if, against the laws of the state, they start preaching their heresies in public, then they are condemned, not for their faith, but as rebels and subverters of society. For it is the oldest law in Utopia that no man's religion should be counted against him. The reasons for the Utopian restrictions are founded on the conviction that those who have no fear except of the law and no hope except for the body will endeavour either openly to break the law or covertly to get round it. But they do not believe that a man's faith can be dictated to him by others, and so they avoid making hypocrites by abstaining from compulsion. Hence the differences in belief do not lead to strife between the sects or to internal disturbances.[3]

Their belief in immortality and in the eternal felicity of man is so firmly fixed that the Utopians may well feel sorrow at a man's illness but never at his death, unless he were to die reluctantly and with fear in his heart, which seems to them a bad augury, as if the departing soul sensed the approach of punishment and were afraid to leave the body. For like the

West Indians of Peter Martyr's description, they believe that rewards and punishments await them after death. They fear lest those who do not gladly run to God may not be welcome to his presence, and so they bury them in silence and with sorrow in their hearts. For those who die merrily, on the other hand, they feel no grief, but accompany the hearse with »joyful singing», whereupon they reverently burn the body and afterwards mark the place with a pillar on which the titles of the deceased are engraved. Then they go home and speak of his virtuous life, and rejoice at his merry death. In this custom they see an encouragement to virtue for the living and a satisfaction for the dead whom they believe to be present with them when they speak about them, although invisible to the imperfect sight of mortals. And since they are firmly convinced of this, their faith prevents them from secretly doing any wrong.[1]

There are two religious orders in Utopia, whose members seek satisfaction in hard work and not in the mere contemplation of God's creation, believing that much labour in this world will gain them felicity in the next. Some tend the sick while others devote themselves to the hardest possible manual labour and gladly perform the most menial duties. One of these orders has adopted celibacy for its members, who have to abstain also from all animal food, while the members of the other eat meat so as to get strong enough for work, and allow marriage in fulfilment of the duty to their country, which instructs them to bear children. The Utopians regard the latter as the more sensible of the two orders, but the former they venerate as the holier. Yet if the members of it founded their asceticism on reason, the Utopians would mock them; since, however, they found it on religion, they honour and respect them.[2]

The priests lead a life »of exceeding holiness, and [are] therefore very few». — This is no expression of dislike of the clergy, as has been commonly supposed, but a deep resignation in the conviction that »the best cannot but be few».[3] — In Utopia there are only thirteen priests in each city and as many churches. The priests are elected, like the magistrates, and afterwards consecrated. They are held in deep reverence. It hardly ever happens that a priest has to be punished for any offence, but if it should occur he is not tried in court, but left to God and his conscience. For the Utopians do not consider it right »to touch him with man's hand, be he never so vicious, which after so singular a sort was dedicated and consecrated to God as a holy offering».[1]

The priests take charge of the moral education of the people. It is their duty to guide the citizens with good counsel in all matters, but punishment is the prerogative of the civil magistrates. The priest may excommunicate a sinner if exhortations prove useless, but the Council alone can impose penalties.[2]

Consistently with the complete equality of the sexes that characterizes Utopian society, women just as well as men can become priests, though »few be chosen». These few are either old or widows. Otherwise the priests are at liberty to marry and then »take to their wives the chiefest women in all their country. For to no office among the Utopians is more honour and pre-eminence given».[3] Their reputation is not confined to their own island only. Seven priests accompany the army in the field, and when the armies engage each other the priests kneel down near by in their vestments and pray »first of all for peace, next for victory of their own part, but to neither part a bloody victory». If their own countrymen pursue the fleeing enemies the priests rush into the thick of the battle to prevent slaughter. The enemy soldiers may seek sanctuary with them; and if they as much as speak to the Utopian priests, »it is enough for the safeguard of their lives»; if they take hold of their vestments, this »defendeth and saveth all their goods from ravine and spoil». It has even happened that when the Utopians have been beaten and in danger of annihilation, the priests »coming between have stayed the murder, and parted both the hosts», enabling their countrymen to conclude peace on equal and just terms. »For there was never any nation so fierce, so cruel and rude, but they had them in such reverence, that they counted their bodies hallowed and sanctified, and therefore not to be violently and unreverently touched.»[4]

This is More's manner of pointing the contrast between Utopia and Europe where not many years before the publication of *Utopia* Pope Julius, riding forth in armour, had led his army to

the siege of Bologna. And before many years more the Eternal
City of Christendom was to be sacked and defiled by the lanceknights committing cruelties unheard-of and indescribable in
decent language, murdering priests and cardinals, while even
the Pope himself only narrowly escaped the fury of the Lutherans
by seeking refuge in his Castle of St. Angelo.

The Utopian churches are large and spacious, and there the
riches of this land of plenty are assembled to the honour of
God. The service is simple, chiefly consisting in a confession of
those general truths about which all sects agree. Each of these
is at liberty to have its own service elsewhere. Before entering
the hallowed place the Utopians confess their faults and forgive
each other, »for they be afeared to come there with troubled
consciences». The entire congregation is clothed in white, and
when the priest enters they fall prostrate as if God himself had
entered among them. Vespucci had said that the most precious
ornaments of the West Indians consisted in variegated birds'
feathers, and in Utopia the vestments of the priests »be neither
embroidered with gold, nor set with precious stones; but they
be wrought so finely and cunningly with diverse feathers of fowls,
that the estimation of no costly stuff is able to countervail the
price of the work». At a sign from the priest the congregation
rise again to their feet. »Then they sing praises unto God»,
and the music, unlike the contemporary church music so full of
artifice, »doth so represent the meaning of the thing, that it
doth wonderfully move, stir, pierce, and inflame the hearers'
minds».

Last they pray to God as the maker of all good and of
themselves. They thank Him because He has granted them to
live in the richest and happiest of all commonwealths and in
the worship of the truest religion, but if there is anything better
and more pleasing to God, then they pray Him of His goodness
to illuminate their minds and guide them to it. But if their
form of government and religious worship is the best possible
one, then they pray God to confirm them in their faith and to
guide others to it, »unless there be anything that in this diversity of religions doth delight his unsearchable pleasure». Then
they pray that after death they may come to Him, but »how

soon or late» they dare not determine. Yet if it be His pleasure, they »would be much gladder to die a painful death and so go to God, than by long living in worldly prosperity to be away from him».[1]

Thus Raphael ends his account of Utopia, emphasizing once more its advantages, and since More knew »he was weary of talking» he abstained from criticism, hoping, he says, for another opportunity of discussion. That opportunity never came. Nor was it part of More's intention. And so he ends the book with the famous remark:

>»In the mean time as I cannot agree and consent to all things that he said; being else without doubt a man singularly well learned, and also in all worldly matters exactly and profoundly experienced; so I must needs confess and grant, that many things be in the Utopian weal public, which in our cities I may rather wish for than hope after.»[2]

X

Against the background, then, of Europe torn by selfish faction and religious strife, More presented a picture of Utopia ruled by law and reason, enjoying freedom from religious persecution. In all fundamentals it must seem a complete contradiction. Instead of private ownership and the enriching of a few at the expense of the many, a communal life where an equal share of plenty comes to the lot of all. Instead of constant warfare, an almost unbroken peace. Instead of tyranny and exaction, the willing collaboration and free consent of all. Instead of a disrupted empire, international amity. Instead of the burning fires of intolerance, toleration and respect for other people's conscience. It was a picture that might indeed appear to be ideal.

A closer examination, however, reveals more similarities than are apparent at first sight. The most obvious of these, and consequently the one selected for vituperation by a captious criticism, is the manner of Utopian warfare. It might seem to the unthinking as if the noble Utopians, when brought into contact with men of flesh and blood, the ideal with reality, might reveal themselves as possessed of the same pitiless brutality, the same innate selfishness, only masked under a veneer of cant and hypocricy. The falsity of such a view becomes immediately obvious if we consider that the outside world with which the Utopians are brought into contact is equally of More's own making. It makes them neither more nor less real than they were. We are still moving in the same world of fiction, subject to the same laws, and we should not forget that it was not part of More's purpose to glorify war but to inculcate a distaste for it. Hence also Utopian warfare must be horrible, so as to constitute an object lesson to his readers and serve European princes as a deterrent from war. But it is necessary to follow the arguments of More's critics.

The second book of *Utopia* was written first, leisurely composed during More's embassy to Bruges in 1515, whereas the first was added after his return to England and only rapidly finished by September 1516.[1] This has led a German historian to the ingenious conjecture that it was only after writing the first book, dealing with the practical problems of the day, that More decided to break the isolation of Utopia and bring it into contact with an outside world. Fresh from the description of the state of English politics, he then set himself the task of showing how the King of England ought to handle the business of foreign affairs and added the account of Utopian warfare and foreign trade, not noticing, however, that in so doing he shattered his own ideal and turned his Utopians into representatives of a policy »more Machiavellian than Machiavelli».[2]

There is no need for so much ingenuity. It might be equally possible that in writing about Utopia in relation to the surrounding world of other fictitious commonwealths — and there are hints in Plato in which he might have sought support for such a venture, were such needed outside the pages of Lucian — More decided to launch on the bolder scheme of direct criticism of Europe in the first book as a supplement to the implied criticism of the second book, and in conscious explanation of it. There is actually nothing in the first book that would necessitate the addition of those chapters, and we have seen how More's inventiveness enabled him to play with new fictions in illustration of his reasoning. The second book of course would have been self-contained without them, but so it would without any other part of the description. The Utopians would have been less complete, that is all. Without the first book, however, the *Utopia* would have been nothing but a *jeu d'esprit*, and the fact that it was written is sufficient testimony to the seriousness of More's purpose The tone of More's Prefatory Letter to Peter Giles may be taken to indicate that even at the time when the second book was only just finished, it was More's intention to add the first, as an explanation and an introduction to the second.

This becomes all the more likely if we look at the manner and tone of the second book. We shall then find that certain habits of the nations of the New World are frankly represented as distasteful. These all occur in connexion with the questions of war and peace on which we know that he felt strongly[1], as if More had found the indirect satire an insufficient instrument for the tune he was playing and so had recourse to that bludgeon which he swings so freely in the first book, in tone and manner reminiscent exactly of these portions of the second. It would in that case be the latter that led directly to the political and social criticism of the first book.

However that may be — and the whole question is but an unfruitful proposition — the passages where our vehement protest is deliberately provoked are exactly those which represent the best likeness to European conditions. Such is the description of the Zapoletes, such the picture of craft, deceit, bribery and corruption, such the account of broken faith in that distant part of the globe.[2] All these episodes, at which More asks us to marvel on account of their incredible strangeness and which he assures us would be unthinkable in Europe[3], are in fact more or less accurate take-offs of European conditions. It has long been recognized that the *Utopia* contains some »wild paradoxes»[4], and the only difficulty has been to decide which they are. But even in his wildest dreams it has never occurred to anybody but Professor Oncken, followed by other German critics, to regard exactly those passages where More most emphatically invites our distaste, as the »Wunschträume ihres Verfassers»[5], and as models consciously set out for his countrymen to copy, down into the most distant future. —

It is quite a different thing that there is a definite likeness in the attitude taken up by the Utopians and the English with regard to foreign nations, to the problems of war and peace and to international relations. Was the *Utopia* not written by one of the most typical as well as one of the greatest of Englishmen? But the likeness does not rest where it has been sought by such critics as these, and to attribute to the fictitious Utopians the same motives which are rightly or wrongly imputed to Englishmen of later generations is unjustified in an historical point of view, and representative of the attitude which I have elsewhere characterized as Machiavellian.

The patent absurdities with which More has seasoned his tale, are even easier to recognize, for their interpretation requires no knowledge of history. I have already referred to the chickens which after the process of artificial hatching follow men and women as if these were their natural parents.[1] Another instance is afforded by the thick chains of gold — manacles more rich than serviceable, I fear — in which the Utopians fetter the most hardened criminals and which have moved Professor Oncken to such eloquent compassion.[2] But is no pity owing to their masters for having to make water in a golden chamber-pot?[3] or are they perhaps to be envied, and was this detail of Utopian comfort one of the »Wunschträume ihres Verfassers«? The Anemolian ambassadors learned a better lesson.[4]

Without allowing ourselves to be deceived by More's manner of alternating seriousness and parody, we may pass from these instances of obvious travesty or patent absurdity to the more fruitful field of the vague kind of likeness that on examination is to be found on almost every page. It is a comparison no more flattering to Europe than the caricatures themselves, lending, as it does, a consistent support to the arguments and accusations of Raphael Hythloday at Cardinal Morton's table in the first book. In the agrarian system of Utopia we may thus recognize a very definite approval of the old system of common land agriculture, which More makes Hythloday so eloquently defend against the enclosures of the new landlords.[5] From the busy making of cloth from wool and flax which occupies the women of Utopia, we may derive support for Raphael's plea in the first book that the old cloth industry of England should be revived and the wool no longer sent to Flanders with all the evil consequences of that trade in the shape of monopolies and rising prices. The general principles of Raphael's suggestions are equally reflected in the reasonable institutions of the Utopians. In their prosperity and happiness lies an affirmation of the age-old view, maintained also by Raphael[1], that the honour of a king consists in the wealth of his subjects, in their obedience to the law a contradiction of the tyrannical thesis that poverty prevents the subjects from rebelling. The Utopian system of condemning criminals to hard labour agrees in principle with Raphael's plea for work instead of hanging and his urgent demand that the poor should be given a chance.

But the likeness is not confined to economics alone. In the right of the Utopians to influence the administration of their commonwealth there lies concealed an earnest defence of the English constitution against the new tyranny of the Tudors. Utopian freedom of speech, limited though it be, has its parallel in More's own determined defence of free speech in Parliament.[2] In their complete freedom of conscience the rights of man are maintained against the new absolutism of the *Prince*, already anticipated in the practice of the European monarchs. In the reluctance of the Utopians to go to war it would not be unreasonable to assume a defence of the peace policy of Henry VII, so rashly abandoned by his son and Wolsey. It is for peace that Hythloday pleads so passionately in the first book, and More himself did not keep his views on the subject to himself.[3] If he chooses France as the butt of his criticism, it is because she was in a similar case, and it was obviously as impossible as it would have been repugnant to More publicly to attack the policy of his own sovereign.

This is exactly the difference between *Utopia* and the *specula principis*, including Erasmus' *Institutio principis Christiani*, that whereas they confined themselves to the restatement of general principles, More in concrete instances exemplifies their application to the practical problems of the day, suggesting means whereby the »evils of states» might be relieved. The *Utopia* must consequently be understood as an argument in favour of the principles of peace, equality and justice, exemplified on the one hand in the Utopian institutions and on the other in their English counterparts, whose continued existence, threatened by the onslaughts of a new age and new ideas, was then under debate. In this light the *Utopia* appears as a protest against the new capitalist system of economics, the new Machiavellian methods in politics, and the spirit of disbelief in religious matters that was rapidly spreading over Europe.

The Utopian confirmation of the immortality of the soul, of the immunity of the clergy and the right of sanctuary, must be taken as More's affirmation of these principles though it is notable that, faithful to his thesis that a reform of the Church must be carried by the Church itself, he says nothing in the first book about the application of these principles in practice. The entire monastic system, endangered by the schemes for the reformation of the Church and the closing of the smaller monasteries, seems to receive a definite sanction in the whole structure of Utopian society. And lest we should remain in doubt, the Utopians are even made to express their unequivocal approbation of these »the rightest Christian companies».[1] It is in instances such as these, that the Utopian counterparts to European institutions are represented as generally attractive and desirable.

In more instances than one we can say for certain what was More's own attitude to the problems under discussion. When the Utopians are made to learn Greek with such alacrity, the address is obviously to the opponents of humanism whom More had later to admonish even in his own university.[2] The Utopian hatred of idleness is paralleled by More's own.[3] The gradation of punishments in the Utopian republic, reserving severer justice for their own subjects and the hardest of all for the magistrates, is part and parcel of More's own outlook, according to which the milder punishment is meted out to the ignorant, the severe to those who ought to know better.[4] The affectionate family life of the Utopians takes us back to his own great house at Chelsea with its busy life of study and profitable occupations, its abhorrence of vice, dicing and gambling.[5] In Utopia, as at Chelsea, the evening meals were introduced by the reading of a short sermon.[6] The uniform Utopian clothing recalls More's preference for simplicity of costume and dislike of gaudy trimmings. The contempt shown by his Utopians for the riches of this world was only equalled by More's own. The reverence of age is an inclination shared by the Utopians and their creator, and the parallelism is carried out on a lower plane in their common toleration of fools.[1] The likeness is brought to the point of self-irony when we are told that the Utopians regard asceticism as »extreme madness», but More has added the saving grace: unless it be »inspired into man from heaven».[2]

While More's idiosyncrasies reflected in the habits of his Utopians add to their humanity, a vague suggestion of a glorified England would cause his countrymen to wonder whether a traveller coming up the Thames with the tide might not one day set foot on London streets as clean, as broad, as magnificently bordered with buildings as those of Amaurote; whether the hygienic arrangements of the Utopians must always remain unattainable to Englishmen; and whether the fifty-three counties of England, with London as the fifty-fourth, might not one day collaborate as whole-heartedly as the fifty-four cities of Utopia and make their island as prosperous. The wish to improve on existing conditions is as obvious in these instances as the criticism on other occasions is pointed, and the likeness must be a stimulus to amelioration. But first of all the Utopian order of law and stability must seem like a vision of paradise to an England that was still undergoing a hard cure of her »wounds of civil war». In all its details Utopia appears as the realization of Hythloday's suggestions in the first book, and against the background of contemporary Europe might be taken to represent the ideal of its creator if it were not for certain difficulties which it is impossible to get round.

XI

In the colonial policy of the Utopians More's German adversaries have found advantageous ground from where to launch their attacks of his supposed imperialism, his prophetic scheme for the exploitation of the world by the British Empire. At first sight one might indeed feel inclined to agree with Professor

Oncken's view that at this point the text shows traces of a later revision.[1] Speaking of the eventuality of an overpopulation in the Island of Utopia, More, in complete agreement with Plato's solution of the same problem in the Laws, makes the Utopians send out colonists to the neighbouring continent, »where the inhabitants have much waste and unoccupied ground». There can be little doubt that Professor Oncken is right in his interpretation of this episode as an expression of More's reaction against Henry's policy of continental conquest and a proposal for colonization.[2] Modern research has confirmed his hypothesis by supplying evidence of More's own interest in, and his father's active support of, his brother-in-law's scheme for settlements in Newfoundland. But that unconquerable warrior of the mind, the late R. W. Chambers, has shown that there need be nothing sinister in this.[3] Cabot and Vespucci had both found á friendly reception among the natives of the new-discovered lands. No blood had as yet flown on the fields of battle in Mexico and Peru. In the new continents vast tracts of land lay unoccupied or very sparsely populated. What could be more natural than the suggestion that work might be provided for the starving unemployed of Europe by means of a colonization of the Western World?

More was not writing a secret and confidential report to the Foreign Office of his own government; he wrote as a free citizen in Latin for all the world to read, and dedicated his book to Peter Giles and Jerome Busleyden, subjects of the Emperor. It was published in all the chief cities of Europe and translated into many languages, but during More's life-time it was neither printed in England, nor translated into English. Whatever practical suggestions it contains are not addressed to an English audience alone, but to the reading public of all Europe. The evils from which England and Europe were suffering, the incessant wars, unemployment, and poverty, so eloquently set out in the first book of *Utopia*, might they not be cured by settling the surplus population overseas? Were not these proposals that might kindle the ambition of a king? It does not seem unlikely that More was trying to divert the attention of the princes of Europe, and that principally of his own king, from the European theatre of war and turn it into a more fruitful channel. There would be no need to seek a minute gain of territory at the expense of one's neighbour if continents lay open to the first comer. There was land there enough for all, as it would seem, even without the necessity of fighting for it.

Neither Rastell nor More was thinking of warlike expeditions. The scheme of his brother-in-law included, it is true, the extension of the King's dominions, but even that bribe to Henry's vanity failed to secure the success of his venture; without it he would scarcely have received even formal permission to pursue his preparations, and even as it was he met not encouragement but official obstruction, resulting in the failure of his plans. His main purpose was to establish a new centre for English trade and a new source of food supply on the shores of Newfoundland where the waters were teeming with fish. As an additional attraction he held out the conversion of the heathen to the Christian faith.[1] There was nothing in these aims of which More need disapprove.

Translated into Utopian terms we find the purpose little changed. The Utopians settle their surplus population in colonies on the waste or sparsely populated land of the neighbouring continent, collaborate »in friendly wise» with the inhabitants, and »so bring the matter about by their laws, that the ground which before was neither good nor profitable for the one nor for the other, is now sufficient and fruitful enough for them both». So far everything seems well. But it would not be Utopia if there were not a crux even here. For

»if the inhabitants of that land will not dwell with them, to be ordered by their laws, then they drive them out of those bounds, which they have limited and appointed out for themselves. And if they resist and rebel, then they make war against them. For they count this the most just cause of war, when any people holdeth a piece of ground void and vacant to no good nor profitable use, keeping others from the use and possession of it, which notwithstanding by the law of nature ought thereof to be nourished and relieved.»[2]

It only remains to mention that if the population at home should decrease and threaten to fall below the statutory limit, the colony is given up and the Utopians return to their own island.

It appears not a little shocking that the peace-loving Utopians should be prepared to go to war, in order to drive others out of the homes which they have occupied before the coming of the Utopians. Nor does it seem consistent with More's teaching. The reason, however, which they give in explanation of their seeming brutality, is as interesting as it is illuminating. As usual the Utopians justify their action by an appeal to justice. »The law of nature» does prescribe that it is unlawful to keep anybody from the use of something of which you have yourself no need. It is of course obvious to anybody that such a law might be abused and turned into a pretext for imperialist expansion. But that is a question of the interpretation of Utopian law, to which we will return presently. In every detail Utopian life and society is regulated by law. The Utopians can be moved to take up arms only in defence of justice. This applies also to Utopian colonization, and their behaviour in this connexion is entirely consistent with their mode of action in other instances. There would consequently be no necessity to assume that the passage was inserted in revision, though it stands a little incongruously in the context. Yet it does nothing to overthrow the order of Utopia, and if Professor Oncken finds it inconsistent with an ideal commonwealth, the only answer is once more that Utopia is not ideal in that sense. The Utopian law is a hard law, but given such laws the Utopian behaviour is neither culpable nor imperialistic. The expansion that takes place, is not made at the expense of any one else but turns to the profit of other nations; whereas its purpose is to provide a means of livelihood for a surplus population. If the previous inhabitants rebel against the profitable order of the Utopians, their rebellion is against the very law of nature, and so they are expelled from their former possessions.

The supposed imperialism of the Utopians can be disproved in every instance. All the reasons for which they go to war can be summed up in the one formula of the maintenance of an international law which applies equally to all nations. In no single instance are the Utopians responsible for the violation of that law. On the contrary, they are the custodians of law and order, in international as well as in home affairs. In their part of the world several nations have recognized this, abstain from aggression and enjoy a partnership in the Utopian economic system which redounds to their own advantage. Only those nations which, inspired by envy of the riches and happiness or the Utopians, attack them, or any other country for that matter, for the sake of gain or conquest, are made to suffer grievous punishment for the breaking of that law. And this applies also if the offence should be directed against the private citizens of any nation, including the Utopians. If therefore the Utopians were to commit a similar offence they would become subject to the same punishment. But since they do not, the question need not arise as to who would impose the sanctions of the law upon them, seeing that the Utopians have become the most powerful of the nations in their part of the world.

This question does not arise because More, who created the Utopians, made them law-abiding, and because with them international law has exactly the same validity as the common law of their own country. The problem has puzzled More's German critics, because to them it seems to be unthinkable that anybody who has the power to break the law would not do so for his own advantage. In the Utopian treatment of the aboriginal population in their colonies, consequently, they have recognized the English attitude towards subject nations of a coloured race, prophetically set out by More as a programme for imperialist expansion. But in this connexion the words of Professor Gerhard Ritter do not seem wholly inappropriate, that »a book must be interpreted according to what it actually says».[1] In Utopia there is no mention of any superiority of the white races. — The racial theory is of an origin altogether different. — Still less do the Utopians think any means justified in their treatment or »inferior coloured races».[2] The accusation levelled against the Utopians of introducing a system of power politics, which it was More's wish to have applied outside Europe, has no foundation in the pages of *Utopia*. The native population in their colonies is granted full rights of citizenship and consequently also the same influence on the administration as the Utopians themselves. There is no dependence of colony on mother country, only the same collaboration that characterizes the relations of all Utopian cities with one another. If, however, the aborigines should turn out to be so given to crime and vice that they cannot live under Utopian law in spite of the manifest advantages it brings them, but »resist and rebel», then they are treated exactly as rebels would be in like circumstances in Utopia, expelled and sent into exile. This case of disciplinary correction falls under the civic code of Utopia, and this may be the reason why colonial wars are not even mentioned in the chapter dealing with war, but in that which relates »Of their living and mutual conversation together».

Neither are the commercial relations with foreign countries, nay, not even the very wars themselves, utilized for the aggrandizement of Utopia or for the acquisition of political power.[1] The Utopians have no more sense of power than desire for private property, and that is as More would have them when he made them. It is not a new observation that power is only attractive to those who want to abuse it; — but when abused it is termed tyranny and violence. To the Utopians power is no easy burden; to them it means trust and responsibility. The trusteeship of law and order with the responsibility of applying the sanctions of the law on those who break it, this is the position that More gave to his Utopians in that part of the world, and they honorably perform their duties without abusing their power in favour of their own interests.

Such is the supposed imperialism of *Utopia*. Whatever More may have thought of it, it must certainly appear as a highly desirable state of affairs, when contrasted with the state of Europe in those days, disrupted by war; the very custodians of temporal and spiritual justice, the wielders of the two swords of Christendom, using their arms not in defence of law and order but to inflame faction and turn it to their own advantage. If the Utopian ideal of international confidence and friendship is to be identified with that of the British Empire and Commonwealth, as German professors would have it, such a comparison can only result in the complete rehabilitation of British methods of indirect rule. Such thoughts, however, were not in More's mind, and we may dismiss this first difficulty as existing only in the minds of his critics. What More may have wished as a

result of his schemes for colonization we may for the moment
confine to the alleviation of the sores of Europe in the cessation
of warfare and the provision of new means of existence for
her poor.

XII

So far the apparent tendency of the *Utopia* seems to agree
tolerably well with what we know of that »righteous and holy
judge» who was its author. But we are not going to escape so
easily. Of all the features of the Utopian commonwealth the
most notable is the community of ownership. Yet we possess
a most emphatic contradiction of the very principle of communism from the pen of More himself. In the *Dialogue of Comfort against Tribulation*, written during his imprisonment in the
Tower, in expectancy of martyrdom, at a moment when he was
opening his heart wholly to God, More wrote:

»But, cousin, men of substance must there be, for else shall you
have more beggars, pardie, than there be, and no man left able to relieve
another. For this I think in my mind a very sure conclusion, that
if all the money that is in this country, were to-morrow next brought
together out of every man's hand, and laid all upon one heap, and
then divided out unto every man alike, it would be on the morrow
after worse than it was the day before. For I suppose when it were
all equally thus divided among all, the best should be left little better
then, than almost a beggar is now. And yet he that was a beggar
before, all that he shall be the richer for that he should thereby
receive, shall not make him much above a beggar still, but many
one of the rich men, if their riches stood but in moveable substance,
shall be safe enough from riches for all their life after.

Men cannot, you wot well, live here in this world, but if that
some one man provide a mean of living for some other many.
Every man cannot have a ship of his own, nor every man be a
merchant without a stock; and these things, you wot well, must
needs be had; nor every man cannot have a plough by himself.
And who might live by the tailor's craft, if no man were able to
put a gown to make? Who by the masonry or who could live a
carpenter, if no man were able to build neither church, nor house?
Who should be makers of any manner cloth, if there lacked men
of substance to set sundry sorts a work? Some man that hath but
two ducats in his house, were better forbear them both and leave
himself not a farthing, but utterly lose all his own, than that some

rich man, by whom he is weekly set a work should of his money lose the one half; for then were himself like to lack work. For surely the rich man's substance is the wellspring of the poor man's living. And therefore here would it fare by the poor man, as it fared by the woman in one of Æsop's fables, which had an hen that laid her every day a golden egg; till on a day she thought she would have a great many eggs at once, and therefore she killed her hen, and found but one or twain in her belly, so that for covetise of those few, she lost many.»[1]

In the course of nearly twenty years that had passed between the writing of *Utopia* and the *Dialogue of Comfort* More might have changed his mind, as Kautsky believed. For a long time that was the accepted view. And in fact, even in his life-time he was charged with inconsistency by Tyndale. The accusation did not concern communism, it is true, but it presents the same problem. Twitting him with the *Encomium Moriae*, written in his house and dedicated to him by his »darling» Erasmus, Tyndale wants to show that More did not always look with any great reverence upon the images and relics of the saints.[2] More answered the charge. After quoting Tyndale's words he writes:

»If this be true, then the more cause have I to thank God for amendment. But surely this is untrue. For, God be thanked! I never had that mind in my life to have holy saints' images or their holy relics out of reverence. Nor, if there were any such thing in *Moria*, that thing could not yet make any man see that I were myself of that mind, the book being made by another man, though he were my darling never so dear. Howbeit, that book of *Moria* doth indeed but jest upon the abuses of such things, after the manner of the disour's part in a play.»[3]

The *Utopia* was not written by another man, but the praises of communism were certainly laid in another man's mouth. Was Raphael Hythloday playing the Jester's part in the comedy of *Utopia*?

How important is the question of interpretation we may gather from the continuation. »In these days», More goes on to say,

»in which men by their own default, misconstrue, and take harm of the very scripture of God, until men better amend, if any man would now translate *Moria* into English, or some works either that I have myself written ere this, albeit there be none harm therein, folk yet being (as they are) given to take harm of that that is good, I would not only my darling's books but mine own also, help to burn them both with mine own hands, rather than folk should (though through their own fault) take any harm of them, seeing that I see them likely in these days so to do.»[1]

More does not repudiate *Utopia*, but times have changed, and he seems to fear lest it should be misinterpreted.

In his *Apology*, published in 1533, when after his resignation he stood alone and in need of making his position clear beyond doubt, there is an interesting passage concerning private ownership, which takes us back at any rate two years nearer the publication of *Utopia*. Refuting the »Pacifyer» who had suggested the confiscation of the superfluous property of the Church, More answers with passion: »But by what right men may take away from any man, spiritual or temporal, against his will, the land that is already lawfully his own, that thing this pacifyer telleth us not yet.»[2] Then More goes on to relate the amusing experiences he has had in making people imagine instances where a change of ownership might seem suitable. At first they had always been enthusiastic, but on second thoughts they had usually had to give up the attempt of introducing a better order of things.

»Not for that we might not always find other enough content to enter into their possessions, though we could not always find other men enough content to enter into their religions, but for that in devising what way they should be better bestowed, such ways as at the first face seemed very good, and for the comfort and help of poor folk very charitable, appeared after upon reasoning, more likely within a while to make many beggars more than to relieve them that are already.»[3]

The argument is the same as in the *Dialogue of Comfort*, and for a more detailed statement of his views on the question of the confiscation of property More refers us to the lengthier argumentation of his own *Supplication of Souls*, which had been published as early as 1530.

More's arguments are chiefly two. One is that no improvement would result if one man's goods were taken away from him and given to other people. The second is that it would be against the law. Remembering with what determination, not to say ferocity even, the Utopians upheld the law, it may be worth while going back to the argumentation which introduces the description of communist Utopia in the first book.

Raphael takes up the question of a redistribution of property, limiting the share of each private citizen and each officer of the crown — even of the king himself, as Fortescue had indeed suggested — to a certain statutory amount. But, he says, this would not solve the problem, for people would start enriching themselves anew and »while you go about to do your cure of one part, you shall make bigger the sore of another part: so the help of one causeth another's harm, forasmuch as nothing can be given to any man, unless it be taken from another».[1] As to the utility of such an attempt there seems to be complete agreement between the opinion voiced by Hythloday and More's own. And in point of law also, surprising as this may seem, there seems to be a considerable amount of unison. For Hythloday says that »here among us, every man hath his possessions several to himself»[2], a statement of fact, comparable to More's phrase concerning »the land that is already lawfully his own», just quoted from the *Apology*. About the legality of this arrangement there is as little doubt in the mind of Hythloday as in More's own. Nor does Raphael even question the justice of it, unless we attribute to his words a meaning which they do not seem to contain. All that he denies is: »that justice is there executed where all things come into the hands of evil men»; and where all except very few are compelled to »live miserably, wretchedly, and beggarly».[3] This is the real problem.

Reasoning in favour of communism, Raphael argues that »where every man under certain titles and pretences draweth and pluckett to himself as much as he can, and so a few divide among themselves all the riches that there is» (the problem in England at that time), »be there never so much abundance and store, there to the residue is left lack and poverty».[4] And, as if he had said that private property is the cause of greed and covetousness, he concludes that »wheresoever possessions be private, where money beareth all the stroke, it is hard and almost impossible that there the weal public may justly be governed and prosperously flourish».[1] He seems to blame the institution of private property for making men evil. More has met that argument in his *Apology,* and he could have contradicted it most emphatically in the *Utopia,* had he wanted to do so.[2] For the sake of argument, however, he lets Hythloday score the point and confines his objections in the dialogue to the utility of communism.

»But I am of a contrary opinion (quod I) for methinks that all men shall never there live wealthily where all things be common. For how can there be abundance of goods, or of anything, where every man withdraweth his hand from labour? whom the regard of his own gains driveth not to work, and the hope that he hath in other men's travails maketh him slothful. Then when they be pricked with poverty, and yet no man can by any law or right defend that for his own, which he hath gotten with the labour of his own hands, shall not there of necessity be continual sedition and bloodshed? specially the authority and reverence of magistrates being taken away; which what place it may have with such men, among whom is no difference, I cannot devise.»

The objection that there would be no respect for authority if all were made equal, is particularly interesting, for More's battle in life was always in defence of authority against the anarchy that was threatening, a defence to which he stuck even on the scaffold. In the dialogue he argues also that the institution of private property may encourage people to virtue, whereas community of goods might lead them to indulge in the sin of slothfulness, thus meeting Hythloday on his own ground, and making the reader forget how he got there. Raphael, however, shows no surprise at these objections. His answer is ready: nobody who has not seen the Utopian commonwealth can know anything about communism, his views are prejudiced and of no validity. And so Raphael tells his story.[3] Yet even at the end the More of the dialogue remains sceptical. »Many things», he says,

»came to my mind which in the manners and laws of that people seemed to be instituted and founded of no good reason, . . . and chiefly, in that which is the principal foundation of all their ordinances, that is to say, in the community of their life and living.»[4]

It must be admitted, I think, that More could not have argued more strongly against communism without destroying his own fiction. We accept it as a potential reality because More tricks us to accept it. Evincing a consummate skill in the manipulation of the dialogue he makes us first accept reason, and not human ability, as the standard by which to judge whether something may be realised or no.[1] Secondly he deliberately deceives us into blaming institutions, instead of human nature, as the cause of abuses and injustice.[2] In this way he persuades us that society can be cured of all the evils besetting it, if only the institutions were reasonable. Raphael Hythloday's argument in favour of »cure» is allowed to get the better of More's own, which is that we should so contrive that »what you cannot turn to good, so to order it that it be not very bad», and which is dismissed by Raphael as effecting at the best no more than a »mitigation» of evil. This is the manner in which More brings about his brilliant *jeu d'esprit*. Without this deception there would have been no Utopia, or if there had, it must have been taken to be More's own ideal.

It is possible to marshal even more arguments against the identification of Hythloday's Utopian fiction with More's practical suggestions for reform. When at the end he says that he must »needs confess and grant, that many things be in the Utopian weal public, which in our cities I may rather wish for than hope after»[3], More uses a phrase *(optarim verius quam sperarim)* which in Humanist terminology means that it would be too good to be true. He expresses it very similarly earlier on when he says that »it is not possible for all things to be well, unless all men were good: which I think will not be yet this good many years».[4] More's »twin spirit» Erasmus had used a similar locution in his *Institutio principis Christiani*, where he said that »it is too much even to hope that all men will be good».[5] And the phrase returns in More's *Apology:* »Would God the world were such as every man were good. . . But sith that this is more easy to wish, than likely to look for». . .[6] the cure is not as simple as that, and does not lie in a change-over from one political system to another.

As for communism it is instructive to glance for a moment at the opinions of other members of that group of humanists whose unison of thought is such that one can often use the words of one to express the ideas of another. In his criticism of the doctrines of the Anabaptists Vives, Erasmus' pupil and More's friend who so warmly recommended the *Utopia*, puts the argument against communism more strongly than either of them, when he protests against »the recent iniquitous wars» and the demand of the rebels for property to be held in common,

»whereas you cannot by any promulgation transfer the virtue of man's mind, or his wisdom, judgment, memory, into common property. Or even if you limit the demand to material things, the taking of the student's books away from him for the use of the soldier will not be recompensed by the student's joint use of the implements of war.»[1]

Erasmus also, speaking on the same subject, says that the communism attempted in practice »was only possible when the Church was small, and then not among all Christians: as soon as the Gospel spread widely, it became quite impossible. The best way towards agreement is that property should be in the hands of lawful owners, but that out of charity we should share one with another.»[2]

During the last years of More's life communism was no joking matter, as indicated in the *Confutation*[3], and when he tackles the problem of how to reconcile private property with Christianity in his *Dialogue of Comfort*, More reaches much the same conclusion as Erasmus though as always he evinces an appreciation of the practical difficulties which escaped his learned friend. And in reading this extract we must not forget that More was »the best friend the poor e'er had».

»But now, cousin, to come to your doubt, how it may be that a man may with conscience keep riches with him, when he seeth so many poor men upon whom he may bestow it; verily that might he not with conscience do, if he must bestow it upon as many as he may. And so must of truth every rich man do, if all the poor folk that he seeth be so specially by God's commandment committed unto his charge alone, that because our Saviour saith, *Omni petenti te, da*, Give every man that asketh thee, therefore he be bounden to give out still to every beggar that will ask him, as long as any penny lasteth in his purse. But verily, cousin, that saying hath (as St. Austin saith other places in Scripture hath) need of interpretation. For as holy St. Austin saith: Though Christ say, Give every man that asketh thee, he saith not yet, give them all that they will ask thee. But surely all were one, if he meant to bind me by commandment, to give every man without exception somewhat; for so should I leave myself nothing.

Our Saviour in that place of the 6th chapter of St. Luke, speaketh both of the contempt that we should in heart have of these worldly things, and also of the manner that men should use toward their enemies. For there he biddeth us love our enemies, give good words for evil, and not only suffer injuries patiently, both by taking away of our good and harm done unto our body, but also to be ready to suffer the double, and over that to do them good again that do us the harm. And among these things, he biddeth us give every man that asketh, meaning, that in the thing that we may conveniently do a man good, we should not refuse it, what manner of man soever he be, though he were our mortal enemy, namely where we see, that but if we help him ourself, the person of the man should stand in peril of perishing. And therefore saith St. Paul, *Si esurierit inimicus tuus, da illi cibum*, — If thine enemy be in hunger give him meat. But now, though I be bounden to give every manner man in some manner of his necessity, were he my friend or my foe, Christian man or heathen; yet am I not unto all men bounden alike, nor unto any man in every case alike. But, as I began to tell you, the differences of the circumstances make great change in the matter.

St. Paul saith, *Qui non providet suis, est infideli deterior*, — He that provideth not for those that are his, is worse than an infidel. Those are ours that are belonging to our charge, either by nature, or law, or any commandment of God.»[1]

In this passage we come extraordinarily near to the meaning of *Utopia* and may be able to judge better of tha: unique consistency which marks More's life and writings. *Utopia* was not a programme either for imperialist expansion, as Oncken would have it, nor for a communist revolution, as Kautsky thought.[2] If it had been understood as a plea for a communist state, would not this have been held against him by his enemies when More stood friendless at his trial? What he actually says in his own person in the dialogue of the first book is that if you want to improve things and influence ministers of state »you must not labour to drive into their heads new and strange informations». You must accept what order you find established and go slow about improving on it, lest you should end by marring rather than mending. This Hythloday admits, inasmuch as he says: »If so be that I should speak those things that Plato feigneth in his weal public, or that the Utopians do in theirs;

these things though they were (as they be in deed) better, yet they might seem spoken out of place.»[1] Even Hythloday does not conceive of communism as a practical programme of reform, but what he has so far pleaded for, is that the greed and luxury of the rich should be restrained, that work should be provided for the poor, that kings should abstain from wars and conquest and seek peace and the welfare of their subjects. These recommendations he wants to push home, and so illustrates them with examples from the history and practice of fictitious peoples like the Polylerites and the Achorians. To More and Peter Giles, however, he tells his story of the happy state of the Utopians, and, the reader's mind being sufficiently prepared to accept the fiction, More publishes Hythloday's story as something »whereby these our cities, nations, countries, and Kingdoms may take example».[2] It was More's manner to teach by means of examples[3], and like a modern Æsop he tells his fables about men instead of animals, but we must not forget that examples may be of various kinds and different application. They may encourage imitation, but they may warn us against it also. Even in the second book of *Utopia* More does not always point the way of the ascent to heaven, but that of the descent also into that hell whose glare flickers over its pages. And so he chose that double manner of praise and parody, making some things good in his ideal commonwealth and some things »very absurd», leaving it to the good sense of his readers to decide where he was in earnest and where he was speaking »in sport».

Returning now to the parallels that it is possible to draw between Utopia and Europe, we find that in the self-abnegating and austere communism of Utopia there lies concealed more than a vague likeness to the Christian monasteries, already threatened by the onslaught of a new age with »new and strange informations».[4] Even more than in the common land agriculture, communism existed in the monasteries of Europe, and so the Utopian example becomes in this light a defence of the monasteries. Where it existed More did not want to see communism abolished, but he did not believe it was possible everywhere in this wretched state of the world. More did not believe in »cure», as did his own Raphael Hythloday, but he regarded it as the duty of all to try and »mitigate» the ills of this world. Nor has he left us in ignorance of the manner in which it should be undertaken.

XIII

The Utopian commonwealth is ingeniously built up from suggestions in the narratives of Vespucci and Peter Martyr, combined with hints from Plato's *Republic* and *Laws*, the *Germania* of Tacitus, and other sources which describe the workings of a primitive society, if by primitive is meant a society living according to the law of nature. All Utopian institutions are founded on reason, and on reason alone. More has been careful never to exceed this self-imposed limitation. The Utopians have learned everything that the ancient philosophers can teach us, and even in their religion there is nothing for which there was no precedent in classical antiquity. Like their institutions, their philosophy and religion also are founded on reason. Their virtue consists in living according to nature, and the law of nature regulates their private and public life, their actions in peace as well as in war. As a synthesis of the best pagan customs and philosophical systems, of the political and religious thought of the pagan world, Utopia is an achievement of no small significance, a *tour de force* which delighted the humanists of the Renaissance and gained for its author a position among the foremost men of learning in Europe, excelling in wit, erudition, and style. To the learned it was not least for its scholarship that *Utopia* became an object of admiration. With a consistency that must impress minds trained in the school of the Platonic Academy of Florence and stimulated by the constructions of Pico and Reuchlin, More assigned to the Utopians a definite place in the order of the universe and in the history of mankind. To the common reader no such complexities need detract from his enjoyment of the book as a production of humanist wit, a *jeu d'esprit* of an uncommonly accessible nature.

Against the background of Europe ruled by Folly, as described by Erasmus in the *Moriae Encomium* or by More himself in the first book, Utopia is described as ruled by Reason. It is a picture that must stimulate even the most unthinking to some searching of heart. As the late R. W. Chambers put it, »the virtues of heathen Utopia show up by contrast the vices of Christian Europe».[1] It is as a plea for Reason that the *Utopia* must strike the reader most forcibly. Against the background of insane tyranny and senseless war, Utopia enjoys both peace and freedom. Instead of lawlessness and anarchy in Europe, law and order in Utopia. It is an order based on respect for the dignity of man and the freedom of conscience, trampled under foot in contemporary Europe. Instead of the selfishness and greed of a few rich men depriving the European masses of their means of livelihood, collaboration for the common good providing plenty for all Utopian citizens. Instead of concentrating on material gains, the Utopians prefer the pleasures of the mind. Learning is there the property of all, whereas in Europe ignorance in the cloak of priesthood was persistently trying to stop the expansion of the mind. In Utopia there is no such contradiction, and, in words strongly reminiscent of Pico[2], More sets out the Utopian conviction of the agreement between the conclusions of an enquiring reason and the truths of a divinely inspired religion.

»For whilst they by the help of this Philosophy search out the secret mysteries of nature, they think that they not only receive thereby wonderful great pleasure, but also obtain great thanks and favour of the author and maker thereof. Whom they think, according to the fashion of other artificers, to have set forth the marvellous and gorgeous frame of the world for man to behold; whom only he hath made of wit and capacity to consider and understand the excellency of so great a work. And therefore, say they, doth he bear more good will and love to the curious and diligent beholder and viewer of his work, and marveller at the same, than he doth to him, which like a very beast without wit and reason, or as one without sense or moving, hath no regard to so great and so wonderful a spectacle.»[3]

Lest, however, we should be misled by the parallel to disapprove of the religious orders as such, More has given Utopia her monks also, who prefer hard manual labour to the contemplation of nature. For even the Utopians recognize that reason is not sufficient for the understanding of all mysteries in nature, and so in their philosophy they call on religion for the

confirmation of the fundamental truths of the existence of God
and man's immortality, postulated by reason. While from the
nature of his sources he had to make his Utopians embrace an
Epicurean doctrine of pleasure which might seem to conflict with
the mediæval ideal of asceticism, More with his supreme intellectual facility dissolves the difficulty by making them recognize
the insufficiency of reason to decide in what the felicity of man
consists and so they come naturally to found morality on religion.

»They reason of virtue and pleasure. But the chief and principal
question is in what thing, be it one or more, the felicity of man
consisteth. But in this point they seem almost too much given and
inclined to the opinion of them which defend pleasure; wherein they
determine either all or the chiefest part of man's felicity to rest.
And (which is more to be marvelled at) the defence of this so dainty
and delicate an opinion they fetch even from their grave, sharp,
bitter, and rigorous religion. For they never dispute of felicity or
blessedness, but they join to the reasons of Philosophy certain principles taken out of religion; without the which, to the investigation
of true felicity, they think reason of itself weak and unperfect.»[1]

It is in the spirit that inspires the Utopian commonwealth
that we must seek the key to the interpretation of its meaning.
This is to be found neither in its laws nor in its institutions.
Utopia is not a country where everybody acts reasonably from
choice only, but under a compulsion intolerable to modern minds.
Utopian law is indeed a law as »ungentle and sharp» as it is
inexorable.[2] To Europe, however, God has given »the new law of
clemency and mercy, under the which he ruleth us with fatherly
gentleness, as his dear children».[3] In our appreciation of Utopia we
must consequently understand that her citizens labour under the
handicap of that »ungentle and sharp law» which reflects their
»grave, sharp, bitter, and rigorous religion», whereas to us Christians God has given not only reason to guide us, but he has also
revealed to us his own law, which is love, and peace, and justice.
»Reason is servant to Faith and not enemy», said More[4],
and so faith rises on the foundations of reason, like the pin-
nacles and spires from the roof of a cathedral. But reason alone
can never arrive at the »fruition of the sight of God's glorious
majesty face to face».[5] To a disciple of St. Thomas Aquinas, Pico,

and Colet, the most elevated pagan philosophy and religion could only be a preparation for the revelation of Christianity[1], and the first rungs on Jacob's ladder. The law of reason, which governs Utopia, is subservient to the Divine law, which ought to rule the behaviour of all Christians. Raphael Hythloday consequently tells us that we must not »wink at the most part of all those things which Christ taught us and so straitly forbade them to be winked at, that those things also which he whispered in the ears of his disciples, he commanded to be proclaimed openly on the house-tops».[2] However ideal it might appear by contrast with the contemporary Europe, Utopia does not represent More's ultimate ideal. It is a state founded only upon reason and ruled by the »ungentle and sharp» law of nature. It does not embody the religion of Christ with its »new law of clemency and mercy». It is a state where slavery is permitted, although in a milder form than in classical antiquity, but it is not a state where all are brethren, as Christ would have it. It is a community where grievous offences against the law are punished with death, but »God commandeth us that we shall not kill».[3]

Reason by itself is »weak and unperfect». Only God's guidance can bring man to the perfection for which He created him. Hence pagan behaviour cannot be a model for Christians to imitate, or as Erasmus put it in his *Institutio principis Christiani*: »Whenever you think of yourself as a prince, remember that you are a Christian prince! You should be as different from even the noble pagan princes as a Christian is from a pagan.»[4] Providence had not granted to the Utopians the privilege of Revelation, and so their manners cannot serve as models for those who have received revealed religion, even if the Utopian welcome extended to the Christians in Hythloday's party seems to indicate that they have not much farther to travel on the road of preparation for the reception of the mystery. So far they remain on the level of pagan philosophy, and the ultimate ideal is very much higher. Speaking of the great princes of antiquity, Erasmus says: »As it would be most disgraceful to be surpassed by them in any honorable deed of theirs, so it would be the last degree of madness for a Christian prince to wish to imitate them without change.»[5] The disgrace of being surpassed

by the heathen was keenly felt by Vives in comparing the
Legenda Aurea with the classical masterpieces of literature, relat-
ing not the lives of saints but of cruel soldiers and generals.[1]
Yet how much greater shame must not we feel, seeing that
whereas we live at constant enmity one against the other, the
Utopians have achieved a state of law and order. In spite of
their hard laws they have surpassed us, not only in the perfection of their institutions, but in their mutual help and
generosity and unreserved collaboration. Even in the instance of
punishments they seem to have surpassed us, for whereas the
Utopians inflict capital punishment only on hardened sinners,
Europeans punish the loss of a little money with »the loss of
man's life».[2] In this manner of interpretation Raphael's arguments in the first book of *Utopia* derive the strongest possible
support from the institutions of the Utopians, not in the likeness
but in the differences between a Christian and a pagan state.
Whereas the pagan Utopians may employ serfs to meet the
needs of labour, the disgrace to Europe is almost inconceivable
inasmuch as servitude in Utopia should be found preferable
to so called »freedom» elsewhere. In attempting to understand
More's meaning we must always remember this, that reason
alone supports the Utopian laws and institutions, but reason has
a claim on Europe also. It is not enemy to Faith, but servant.
In the likeness of Utopia More shows how certain institutions
in Europe, threatened by destruction, are founded on reason and
so worth preserving, because where there is reason there is hope
of religion. But for Christians to try and imitate Utopian institutions without change »would be the last degree of madness».

When therefore sociologists are concerned to show to what
extent the Utopian ideal has been realised in modern society
and to what degree it still remains unfulfilled, they are merely
breaking up the Coloseum in order to build the Farnese Palace.
They have seen only the stones and forgotten the vision. It was
not the constitution of commonwealths that More desired to reform, but the spirit. The Utopian institutions can be nothing
except »very absurd» without the spirit that informs them. They
must not be copied, but surpassed by Christian institutions.
The community of goods that reason recommends to the Utop-

ians, must be excelled in the spiritual community of all Christians. It was the Christian monasteries that provided the pattern for the Utopian republic, and in More's mind it was they that represented the mundane revelation of the ultimate ideal.

It might be exemplified in concrete instances how far short of the Christian standard the Utopians actually fall. When the priests in Utopia are allowed to marry, this must not be understood as More's scheme for the reformation of the Church; it is merely that God has not granted them that personal intimacy which has only been made possible through the Incarnation. Utopian religious customs are no more models for the Christian Church than are the political institutions of that commonwealth, and so must not be taken literally.[1] The fact that in Utopia God is worshipped under different names, is certainly not served up by More for imitation by the Catholic Church, to which in More's view God had alone revealed himself. The Utopians with reason as their sole guide can only convince themselves of the existence of God; about his nature they can know nothing. Hence toleration is natural to them. Yet I cannot agree with those who would have it not apply where Christianity is concerned, being a revealed religion and so admitting of no doubt as to the truth of its doctrine.[2] The Divine law is a law »of clemency and mercy», and the Utopian toleration requires its counterpart in Christian charity.[3] Whatever ideas he may have entertained concerning the reformation of the Church, and it would carry us too far to go into the question of its details, More left it to the Church itself. Even in the first part of *Utopia* where he so sharply criticizes European conditions, not sparing ecclesiastics any more than laymen, it is the abuses he condemns, not the institutions. What he is asking for, is that in the same way as reason was allowed to regulate life in Utopia, so reason illuminated by Divine revelation should be given a hearing in European affairs. Just as the Utopians live in strict obedience to the law of nature, so must we be ruled by the law of Christ.[4] Temporal justice is »the strongest and surest bond of a commonwealth», says More[5], and he does not want us to set it aside, but man-made law must be tempered by the law of Christ which is itself the highest justice[6].

Such has long been the Roman Catholic interpretation of *Utopia*, and it has been convincingly restated during recent years.[1] It has been maintained with characteristic vigour and eloquence by the late R. W. Chambers in his great biography of More. This was also the way in which his contemporaries understood More's intention, as plainly appears from Budé's remark that if only the three principles of Utopia, which he accurately defined as equality, love of peace, and contempt of gold, could be »fixed in the minds of all men, ... We should soon see pride, covetousness, insane competition, and almost all other deadly weapons of our adversary the devil, fall powerless.»[2] By showing how far short of the Utopians contemporary Europe fell in the practice of the four cardinal virtues of wisdom, fortitude, temperance, and justice, More wanted to stimulate us not only in the exercise of mundane virtue but of the Christian virtues also of faith, hope, and charity. In St. Augustine's terminology we may say that in Utopia More gives us such a description of a *vita socialis*, based only on the four pagan virtues, as must most forcibly remind us of our duty by means of an ardent exercise of the three Christian virtues to prepare for the *Civitas Dei*. Self-love, according to St. Augustin, is the opposite to the love of God, and so it is the love of self in all its utterances from mere vanity to cruel tyranny that More attacks most violently in the first book of Utopia, showing us in the second how the noble Utopians have eschewed self from all their dealings and find their greatest pleasure in working for the good of all and in actively helping their fellows. We cling to our worldly treasure, but the Utopians gladly give up their houses every ten years. More does not want us to imitate this custom, which no doubt he would have described as »very absurd», but he did want us to feel that one house is »as nigh heaven» as another.[3] More did not want us to give everything away, but he did want us to use our wealth in such a way that it should not be said that in our states »money beareth all the stroke»[4]; not for the increase of our own luxury, but for the relief of poverty, so that the prosperity of our society might rival that of Utopia itself. The love of power, which in the guise of the new Machiavellian statecraft was ruining Europe, was in More's view but another outcome of the love of self. In Utopia, however, aggressors are so cruelly punished that they are not likely to disturb the peace a second time.

Religion must reinforce the arguments of reason and Christian society surpass the pagan. It is not our institutions that we must destroy, but those evil passions which are at the root of the abuses. More's programme of reform was one of personal amelioration. »There is nothing better», John Colet, his teacher and confessor, had written to Erasmus, »than that we should lead a pure and holy life, which in my judgment will never be attained but by the ardent love and imitation of Jesus».[1] Had not St. Matthew told us also, that »the disciple is not above his master, nor the servant above his lord». More had not forgotten the lesson[2], and his own passion bears witness to his pious striving to imitate his Master.

In his *Apology* More did not omit pointing to the personal responsibility of each individual for the good of all. Speaking of the »faults, enormities, and errors»[3] that beset both state and church, he says these he would wish to have amended, »and every man specially labour to mend himself»[4]. This is the advice also that Raphael Hythloday would have wished to give his king — to »let him rather amend his own life, renounce unhonest pleasures, and forsake pride».[5] And in the next instance More asks all to work together to eliminate the faults of society, »observed in the doing evermore such order and fashion as may stand and agree with reason and justice, the king's laws of the realm, the Scripture of God, and the laws of Christ's Church, ever keeping love and concord. . . . This has been hitherto the whole sum of my writing.»[6] Neither did More neglect to rub in the lesson, »for I think every man's duty toward God is so great, that very few folk serve him as they should do».[7]

If, then, one should want to sum up the *Utopia* in a few inadequate words — for the subject is interminable — one may say that:

In the first book More analyses the evils that beset early sixteenth century English society — and to some extent these are the evils of all human society — and makes suggestions how they might be mitigated. The second book is a moral fable, intended to delight with its wit and ingenuity while it teaches a lesson in private and public morals by means of an example. It does not describe the ultimate ideal, but one that is practicable enough, which we are asked not slavishly to copy, but to surpass and excel. The *Utopia* does not attempt a final solution of the problems of human society — for More was too wise to attempt the impossible — but it contains an appeal addressed to all of us, which allows of no refusal, that we should try and do each one his share to mend our own selves and ease the burden of our fellow-men, to improve mankind and prepare for the life to come. In this lies its enduring power, that however high we may fix the ideal, to whatever perfection we may attain, More points higher still, from matter to the spirit, and from man to God.

NOTES

Page 1.

[1] P. S. Allen, *Opus epistolarum Des. Erasmi Roterodami*, 8 vols., Oxford, Clarendon Press, 1906—34, vol. II, No. 499, p. 414. Translated by F. M. Nichols, *The Epistles of Erasmus from his earliest letters to his 51st year*, 3 vols., London, Longmans, Green & Co., 1901—18. The passage is here quoted from E. M. G. Routh, *Sir Thomas More and his Friends*, Oxford University Press, 1934, p. 78, without other alterations than that of »Sovereign» into »prince», which seems to me better to conform with the Utopian constitution, and of »puerile» to »childish» for no reason except personal preference.

Page 2.

[1] P. S. Allen, l. c.

[2] *The Utopia of Sir Thomas More*, ed. J. H. Lupton, Oxford, Clarendon Press, 1895, pp. 177—80.

[3] Letter to John Holt, Nov. 1501, *Anglia* XIV, 1891—2, p. 499.

[4] O. E. D.

[5] As an instance may serve the following quotation from *The Times* 28 Jan. 1942: »The other essential conditions for the success of the idea of the Balkan Federation are considered to be: That all the Balkan countries should give up their Utopian yearnings for the creation of huge empires at the expense of their neighbours and should realise that the Balkans are not fit for imitation Bismarcks or Fredericks;» etc. But Utopia was no place for conquerors, and yearnings for empire should not be branded as Utopian.

[6] *An Englishman Looks at the World.* »About Sir Thomas More.»

Page 3.

[1] E. g. Letter to Erasmus 3 Sept. 1516, Allen, vol. II, No. 461, p. 339. For a further discussion of the name, see *Notes and Queries*, 7th series, vol. V, pp. 101—2, 229—31, and 371.

[2] Letter to Lupset, prefixed to the Paris edition of *Utopia*, 1517; reprinted Lupton, p. lxxxvii.

[3] E. g. Karl Kautsky, *Thomas More und seine Utopie. Mit einer historischen Einleitung*, Stuttgart 1887; Helen Taylor, *Sir Thomas More on the Politics of To-Day*, Fortnightly Review 1870, pp. 125—37. Cf. also the present writer's *Thomas Mores Utopia som samhällsideal*. Föredrag hållet inför the Westermarck Society 20. 11. 1942. Åbo 1943; and *Medeltida förebilder till en internationell fredsorganisation* in *Eros och Eris; kulturessäer till-*

ägnade Rolf Lagerborg, Helsingfors, Söderström, 1944. I regret not having had access either to W. E. Campbell, *More's Utopia and his Social Teaching*, London 1930, or to R. O'Sullivan, *The Social Theories of Sir Thomas More*, Dublin Review, July 1936.

[4] J. O. Hertzler, *The History of Utopian Thought*, London 1922, p. 281.

[5] Cf. H. G. Wells, *Outline of History*, II, p. 211.

[6] V. e. g. L. von Stein, *Geschichte der socialen Bewegung in Frankreich von 1789 bis auf unsere Tage*, 3 vols., Leipzig 1850; F. Engels, *Die Entwicklung des Socialismus von der Utopie zur Wissenschaft*, 4th ed. Berlin 1891; H. de B. Gibbins, *English Social Reformers*, London 1892; A. Dietzel, *Beiträge zur Geschichte des Socialismus und Kommunismus. Morus' Utopien und Campanellas Sonnenstaat*. Vierteljahrschrift für Staats- und Volkswirtschaft 5, 1897, pp. 217—38 and 372—412; A. Lichtenberger, *Le socialisme utopique*, Paris 1899; G. Henrikson-Holmberg, *Socialismen i Sverige 1770—1886*, Stockholm 1913; Hertzler, op. cit.; and Karl Vorländer, *Von Machiavelli bis Lenin. Neuzeitliche Staats- und Gesellschaftstheorien*, Leipzig 1926.

Page 4.

[1] Cf. Alfons Erb, *Thomas Morus. John Fisher*, Freiburg i. Br. 1935, p. 93 n.

[2] For convenient bibliographies, v. Friedrich Kleinwächter, *Die Staatsromane*, Vienna 1891; Walter Bagley's bibliography in his ed. of *Nova Solyma*, New York 1902; Emilie Schoman, *Französische Utopisten und ihr Frauenideal*, Berlin 1911; and Yrjö Hirn, *Ön i världshavet*, Helsingfors 1928. Cf. also Hermann Ullrich, *Robinson und Robinsonaden: Bibliographie, Geschichte, Kritik*, Weimar 1898. The present writer regrets not having had access to G. E. Dermenghem, *Thomas More et les utopistes de la renaissance*, Paris 1927.

[3] Cf. also I. Vennerström, *Svenska utopister* i *Den svenska socialismens historia*, Stockholm 1913.

Page 6.

[1] The contemporary translation of the Latin »passim». For a bibliography, v. *Utopia*, ed. G. Sampson and A. Gutkelch, London 1910.

[2] The Swedish translation is by Carl Elof Svenning, with a preface by Alf Ahlberg, Federativs bibliotek, I, 1930.

Page 8.

[1] E. g. J. H. Lupton, v. supra, and V. Michels and Th. Ziegler's ed. of the Latin text, Berlin 1895.

[2] Thomas More, *L'Utopie ou le traité de la meilleure forme de gouvernement*. Texte latin édité par Marie Delcourt avec des notes explicatives et critiques. Paris, Librairie E. Droz, 1936.

[3] In an interesting appendix Mme. Delcourt gives a list of the rare words used by More, pp. 213—16.

[4] Op. cit. p. 29.

Page 9.

[1] Professor Eli Heckscher informs me that he actually adopted the word in his history of *Mercantilism* (English edition 1935) and that it is now commonly employed in economic literature.

[2] Delcourt, pp. 29—31.

[3] Letter to Ulrich von Hutten, 23 July 1519, Allen, IV, No. 999, p. 21.

[4] For instances, v. Delcourt, p. 28 sq.

[5] Ibid.

Page 10.

[1] E. g. J. Churton Collins in his edition of Robinson's translation, Oxford, Clarendon Press, 1904; and Mgr. Philip E. Hallett in his modernized edition of the same, London, Burns Oates & Washbourne, 1937.

[2] Unrivalled among these the late R. W. Chambers, whose *Thomas More* was published by Cape in 1935. It has left in these pages more than one mark of unacknowledged indebtedness, of which the present writer is nevertheless deeply sensible.

[3] Cf. the well-known passage in *The Confutation of Tyndale's Answer, English Works of Sir Thomas More*, 1557, pp. 422—3; quoted e. g. Mgr. Hallett, op. cit., pp. 64—5 n. V. infra p. 67 sq.

[4] »Ridet aether; exultat terra.» Mountjoy to Erasmus, 27 May 1509, Allen, I, No. 215, p. 450.

Page 11.

[1] A. F. Pollard, *Wolsey*, Longmans Green & Co., 1929, p. 81.

[2] Lupton, p. 51. I modernize the spelling throughout. The Latin text is always to be found on the same page.

Page 12.

[1] Ibid. pp. 299—300 and 303.

[2] P. 301.

[3] Passim, e. g. *Institutio principis Christiani*, transl. L. K. Born, Records of Civilization, Columbia University Press 1936, pp. 216 and 225.

[4] *Annotations to the Pandects* and *De asse*, v. Börje Knös, *Guillaume Budé och den franska humanismens renässans*, Svenska Humanistiska Förbundet, No. 48, Stockholm 1939, pp. 67 and 91 sq.

[5] V. spec. *De subventione pauperum.*

[6] Sir John Fortescue, *The Governance of England*, ed. C. Plummer, Oxford 1885, p. 141. As Lord Chancellor More, on the contrary, tried to temper the rigour of the law. V. Roper's *Life of More*, ed. Elsie V. Hitchcock, E. E. T. S. 1935, p. 45.

[7] »Item, we se dayly, how men þat have lost thair godis, and be ffallen into pouerte, be comme anon robbers and theves; wich wolde not haue ben soche, yff pouerte hade not brought them þerto.» Op. cit. p. 140.

[8] Lupton, p. 58.

[9] Ibid., p. 61.

[10] P. 60.

Page 13.

[1] P. 63.

[2] Pp. 64—73. Erasmus also believed that capital punishment should only be used in the last resource if other correctives failed. (*Institutio principis Christiani*, Born, pp. 224—5.) I am of course well aware that More does not make the suggestion in his own person, but I am equally convinced that the cautious empirical attitude of Morton in the dialogue closely corresponds to that of More himself, always careful to consider each case on its own merits.

[3] Lupton, p. 57.

[4] A. F. Pollard, op. cit., p. 85. Cf. also *The Domesday of Enclosures 1517—18*, ed. I. S. Leadan, Royal Historical Society, 1897. In 1549 popular anger against the enclosures led to serious riots, involving most of central, eastern and south-western England. (Charles Sturge, *Cuthbert Tunstal*, Longmans Green & Co., 1938, p. 282.) More has been accused of reversing Wolsey's policy. Actually he pronounced judgment according to law and the merits of the case.

[5] Lupton, p. 58.

[6] Ibid. pp. 56—7. It is instructive to compare the general practice of dismissing servants by the hundred without notice with More's own anxiousness to provide for his servants on the occasions when he was forced to reduce his staff. V. letter to his wife, 3 Sept. 1529: »And whether ye think it good that we so shall do or not, yet I think it were not best suddenly thus to leave it all up and to put away our folk of our farm, till we have somewhat advised us thereon. Howbeit, if we have more now than ye shall need and which can get them other masters, ye may then discharge us of them. But I would not that any man were suddenly sent away, he wot not whither.« (*English Works*, 1557, p. 1418; reprinted in *Selections from the English Works*, ed. P. S. and H. M. Al'en, Oxford, Clarendon Press, 1924, p. 163.) Cf. *A Dialogue of Comfort against Tribulation*, ed. Mgr. P. E. Hallett, Burns Oates & Washbourne 1937, pp. 170—2; and Stapleton, *Tres Thomae*, III, translated by Mgr. Hallett, Burns Oates & Washbourne 1928, p. 158.

[7] Lupton, pp. 55—7.

[8] Ibid. p. 92. Cf. also Fortescue: »Item, hit is the kyngis honour, and also is office, to make is reaume riche; and it is dishonour whan he hath but a pouere reaume, off wich men woll say þat he reigneth but vppon beggers.« (Op. cit., p. 139.)

[9] Cf. Budé's complaints in his letters and his exhortations in *L'instruction du prince* (Knös, pp. 113 and 134) and More's letter to Wolsey 20 Sept. 1523, where in answer to the Duke of Bourbon's suggestion that the English army should »in the marching proclayme libertie sparing the cuntre fro burnyng and spoile, the kinges highnes thinketh that sith his army shall march in hard wether wᵗ many sore and grevouse incommoditees if they shold also forbere the profite of the spoile the bare hope whereof, though

88

they gate litle, was great encoraging to theym they shall have evill will to march far forward and theyre capitayns shall have mych a doo to kepe theym from crying: home, home!» (Joseph Delcourt, *Essai sur la langue de Sir Thomas More*, Paris, H. Didier, 1914, p. 343 sq. The punctuation is the present writer's. The letter is summarized by J. S. Brewer in *Letters and Papers, Foreign and Domestic*, III, ii, p. 1392.)

Page 14.

[1] Lupton, p. 87.
[2] *History of Richard III, English Works*, ed. W. E. Campbell, I, 1931, p. 70 F.
[3] Lupton, pp. 85—7.
[4] Hermann Oncken points to the versified *Libell of Englyshe Polycye*, 1436 (ed. Sir G. Warner, Oxford 1926) and Sir John Fortescue's treatises. (Introduction to Gerhard Ritter's translation of *Utopia*, Berlin, Reimar Hobbing, 1922, p. 24.)

Page 15.

[1] For other sources, see e.g. R. H. Tawney and E. Power, *Tudor Economic Documents*, Longmans Green & Co., 1924; *Letters and Papers*, the Chronicles of Wriothesley and Hall, and by modern writers J. A. Froude, *The Reign of Henry VIII*; J. S. Brewer, *The Reign of Henry VIII*; A. F. Pollard, *Henry VIII and Wolsey*; H. A. L. Fisher, *The Political History of England*, V; G. M. Trevelyan, *English Social History*, Longmans Green & Co., 1944. See also the numerous contemporary documents referred to by annotators such as Lupton and Churton Collins. Nor should John Richard Green's *Short History of the English People* be forgotten.
[2] Allen. IV, No. 999, p. 21. I use Allen's translation in the *Selections from the English Works* of More, p. 8.
[3] For conditions in Germany, v. Kautsky, op. cit., Introduction.
[4] Apart from the commendatory epistles, see among innumerable contemporary references the recommendations of Erasmus in his Paraphrase of the Romans, Louvain 1517, and of Vives both in the Plan drawn up for the studies of Princess Mary and in *De tradendis disciplinis* (Foster Watson, *Vives: On Education*, Cambridge University Press, 1913, pp. lxxv and 160).

Page 16.

[1] *Luciani compluria opuscula ab Erasmo & Thoma Moro in latinorum lingua traducta*, Paris 1506 and 1514, Venice 1516 and 1517, Basle 1528. More's share consisted in the translations of Cynicus, Menippus seu Necromantia, Philopseudes seu incredulus, Tyrannicida with the Declamatio Mori de eodem.
[2] Mme. Delcourt points to Iamboulos' journey to the sun in Diodorus Siculus as a possible source. (Op. cit. p. 18.)

[3] Lupton, p. 33. Parodies of Maundeville are found elsewhere, e. g. the description of the country of the Polylerites (»talkers of much nonsense») p. 65.

[4] Ibid. p. 25 sq.

Page 17.

[1] P. 28. Cf. *The Cosmographiae Introductio of Martin Waldseemüller in Facsimile. Followed by the Four Voyages of Amerigo Vespucci*, etc. Ed. J. Fischer and F. von Wieser, U. S. Catholic Historical Society, No. IV, New York 1907, p. 91 sq.

[2] More's championship of Greek studies in *Utopia* has been ably elucidated by Christopher Hollis, *Sir Thomas More*, Sheed & Ward 1934, pp. 73—5.

[3] For the humanist ideal of quiet conversation in the open air, v. J. Huizinga, *Erasmus*, deutsch von Werner Kaegi, Basle 1928, pp. 110—111.

[4] Cf. Marie Delcourt, op. cit., p. 27.

[5] Cf. R. W. Chambers, op. cit., p. 123.

[6] Rafael Karsten, *Inkariket och dess Kultur*, Helsingfors, Söderström, 1938, p. 30.

[7] Lupton, pp. 31—2.

[8] Ibid. p. 34.

Page 18.

[1] Cf. *English Works*, Campbell, II, 1931, p. 127 B, and Cresacre More, *The Life of Sir Thomas More*, 1726, p. 179.

[2] Lupton, p. 274.

[3] Cf. More's letter to Peter Giles, Lupton, p. 7, and the second hoaxing letter prefixed to the Paris edition of 1517, translated by Mgr. Hallett in his edition of *Utopia*, pp. 23—6.

[4] *English Works*, Campbell, I, pp. 1—20.

[5] The references are too numerous to list since More was constantly rubbing it in, but v. spec. *The Four Last Things* and the *Dialogue of Comfort*.

[6] Lupton, pp. 35—6.

[7] More's *English Works*, Campbell, I, p. 14 sq.

[8] E. g. Huizinga, op. cit., p. 111. Though newly appointed to the Council of Charles, later Emperor, Erasmus never served in that capacity.

[9] More to Erasmus, Feb. 1516, Allen, II, No. 388, p. 196 sq.

[10] More to the same, Oct. 1517, Allen, III, No. 688, p. 111.

[11] Cf. e. g. Busleyden's letter to More, Lupton, p. 314 sq.; Vives' letter to the Town Council of Bruges prefixed to *De subventione pauperum* 1526, and *De tradendis disciplinis*, Foster Watson, p. 283. More's own career is witness to his consciousness of the fact that, in the words of Vives, the fruit of all our studies is to apply them to the common good.

[12] Lupton, p. 37 sq.

[13] Ibid. p. 39.

Page 19.

[1] Pp. 41—3.

[2] Pp. 43, 59, 71, and 72.

[3] Pp. 39—40.

Page 20.

[1] Pp. 88—92. For contemporary examples of the practices mentioned, v. notes in the editions of Lupton and Churton Collins.

[2] Cf. More's Epigram: *Populus consentiens regnum dat et aufert* in *Epigrammata Thomae Mori pleraque e Graecis versa*, Basle 1518 and 1520; reprinted in *Lucubrationes*, Basle 1563, and *Opera omnia*, Louvain 1565 and 1566, and Francfort 1689. Cf. also Erasmus' saying that »kingly authority is service, not tyranny» (*Institutio principis Christiani*, Born, p. 168). Sir John Fortescue quoted with approval the dictum of St. Thomas Aquinas: »Rex datur propter regnum, et non regnum propter regem.» (*The Governance of England*, p. 127.)

[3] Cf. *Holy Bible*, passim (Mgr. Hallett gives a number of references, p. 78 n.); and Plato, *Republic*, I, xvi—xvii. The simile recurs in the writings of Xenophon and numerous mediæval writers on statecraft. Only a German critic, Heinrich Brockhaus, has seen in it a reference to the Pope, shepherd of all Christians, and believes that the *Utopia* was written by Erasmus from the account of the Bishop of Bari in criticism of the Vatican and in praise of the monasteries of Mount Athos. He even adduces as evidence a modern Baedeker in the attempt to prove that the »populivorous» sheep of Hythloday's account must be the ravenous sheep of the Roman Campagna. (*Die Utopia-Schrift des Thomas Morus erklärt von Heinrich Brockhaus*, Beiträge zur Kulturgeschichte des Mittelalters und der Renaissance, No. 37, Leipzig and Berlin 1929, pp. 14 and 20.) More was to use the same simile again in his speech in Parliament after Wolsey's fall. (Chambers, op. cit., p. 241.)

[4] Cf. *The Apologye of Syr Thomas More, Knyght*, ed. I. A. Taft, E. E. T. S. 1930, p. 58 sq.; and infra p. 82.

[5] Lupton, pp. 92—7.

[6] Ibid. p. 81.

[7] Pp. 81—4. For the historical events referred to, v. notes of Lupton and Churton Collins.

[8] Lupton, p. 85.

Page 21.

[1] Ibid. pp. 84—7. Cf. similar views expressed by Erasmus in the contemporary *Institutio principis Christiani*, Born, pp. 240 and 247.

[2] Lupton, p. 79 sq. Cf. Vives' Dedication of *De tradendis disciplinis* to King John III of Portugal where he expresses similar views on the advantages of collaboration between princes and scholars. (Foster Watson, p. 5.)

[3] Lupton, p. 80 sq. Cf. Plato, *Republic*, V, xviii. Referring to the books of philosophers More was probably thinking also of the *specula principis*

of which the most recent had been Erasmus' work, published only six months before *Utopia*, the outcome to no little extent of conversations with More. I do not note all the parallels.

⁴ Second letter to Peter Giles, Hallett, p. 24.

⁵ Lupton, pp. 97—9.

⁶ Ibid. pp. 99—100.

Page 22.

¹ *English Works*, Campbell, I, p. 70 G; modern version p. 454.

² *Dialogue Concerning Tyndale* in *English Works*, Campbell, II, p. 225 B. Cf. also More's second letter to Peter Giles, Hallett, p. 24, and *Apology*, p. 74.

³ Lupton, p. 100. Cf. *Apology*, p. 189, and Erasmus, *Institutio principis Christiani*, Born, p. 143.

⁴ Cf. also Plato, *Laws*, 736 D, and Erasmus, op. cit., pp. 211 and 213.

⁵ Lupton, pp. 100—101.

⁶ Ibid. p. 103 sq.

⁷ P. 107 sq.

⁸ P. 109.

⁹ Ibid. The manner, however, in which Hythloday arrives at this conclusion should be noted, for he does it by deliberately identifying a country where »possessions be private» with one »where money beareth all the stroke» (p. 104).

Page 23.

¹ Pp. 109—10.

² Pp. 110—14.

³ Introduction to *Utopia* in translation by Gerhard Ritter, Berlin, Reimar Hobbing, 1922, p. 24 (I refer to this essay as »Introduction»); *Die Utopie des Thomas Morus und das Machtproblem in der Staatslehre,* Sitzungsberichte der Heidelberger Akademie der Wissenschaften, Philosophisch-historische Klasse, 1922, p. 10 (I refer to this lecture as »Heidelberger Akademie»).

⁴ Letter to Erasmus, Feb. 1516, Allen, II, No. 388, p. 196 sq.

⁵ *English Works*, Campbell, I, p. 14 sq.

Page 24.

¹ Erasmus to Hutten, Allen, IV, No. 999, pp. 20 and 22. I use the translation furnished by Allen in *Selections from the English Works* of More, pp. 7 and 9.

² *Cosmographiae Introductio*, p. 134.

³ Gerhard Ritter, *Machtstaat und Utopie*, Munich and Berlin, 1940, p. 63. V. the present writer's review, *Historisk demonologi*, Finsk Tidskrift, Aug. 1941, pp. 16—27. It is notable, however, that while enlarging on most of his other ideas, Ritter objects to Oncken's definition at this point and prefers describing the less attractive aspects of the Utopian commonwealth as the »Wunschträume ihres Verfassers». (V. p. 72.)

⁴ »Durch die Maske des Raphael spricht hier Erasmus von Rotterdam.«
(Ferdinand Geldner, *Die Staatsauffassung und Fürstenlehre des Erasmus
von Rotterdam*, Historische Studien, Heft 191, Berlin 1930, p. 179. Cf.
also p. 55.)

⁵ *Republic*, I, 347, and VII, 520. Like Cicero and St. Augustine, Erasmus also approved of the definition (op. cit., p. 160).

⁶ E. g. Roper, p. 25; and Harpsfield's *Life of Sir Thomas More*, ed.
E. V. Hitchcock, E. E. T. S. 1932, p. 95.

Page 25.
¹ Ritter, op. cit., p. 164: »Über den Sinngehalt eines Werkes entscheidet
aber in letzter Instanz nicht das, was sein Urheber damit gemeint haben
könnte, oder was er damit hat ausdrücken wollen, sondern der Sachzusammenhang dessen, was er wirklich gesagt hat. Denn das fertige Werk steht unabhängig von seinem Autor da.« Hardly less startling is the thesis maintained
by Dr. Michael Freund (*Zur Deutung der Utopia des Thomas Morus. Ein
Beitrag zur Geschichte der Staatsräson in England.* Historische Zeitschrift
142, 1930, pp. 254—78) that a historical and political interpretation of *Utopia*
need only consider what he calls the »objective significance« of More's
work. According to this method the »real content« of *Utopia* should
be sought in connexion with »den historischen Lebenskräften Englands«,
but quite apart from the subjective meaning of his writings and his personal
character. By means of this method the identification of the ideology of
Utopia with the Irish policy of Cromwell that resulted in the massacre of
Drogheda becomes justified. The reservation against imputing the same
motives to More as to the Lord Protector is as naive as the whole thesis
(pp. 258—9).

Any refutation of similar stuff would be gratuitous but for the fact that
recent intellectual movements in Germany, parading under the high-falutin
banners of »Ideengeschichte« and »Ideenanalyse«, busy themselves with
exactly such speculations. Yet a simple comparison will show up the
fundamental mistake, involved in the method itself. Ideas can only be
understood by means of the words and sentences in which they are expressed, and a word fulfills a function in the sentence parallel to that of
an idea in a larger sequence. Now it should be obvious that since a word
derives its meaning from the context and, placed in a different context,
acquires a different meaning — this is the simplest of all semantic rules —
it cannot be used indiscriminately in different connexions without altering
its sense. But no more can an idea be arbitrarily taken out of one sequence and introduced into another without suffering distortion. And an
idea, considered apart from its subjective meaning, can have no other
significance than the vague connotation of a word in the dictionary.
Dangerous as such a method must always be in consequence (cf. the wise
words of Prof. Huizinga concerning the widely varying contents of historical
ideas, *Im Bann der Geschichte*, Burg-Verlag, Basle 1943, p. 39), it can only
be successful if the most scrupulous care is exercised in ascertaining the

particular meaning of an author in each case. In *Utopia*, however, we are not concerned with a philosophic system but with a fanciful accumulation of such thoughts and customs as More chose to attribute to his Utopians because he thought them consistent with reason and pagan manners. Consequently an analysis of the functions of such thoughts must be based on a comparison between his sources and his known views and conjectured intentions. Only when his own meaning has been ascertained, can his ideas be placed in their historical context without suffering distortion. Without such precautions ideas may well be attributed to him for which only his critics are responsible.

If Dr. Freund's criticism of *Utopia* mirrors his own mind rather than More's, his conception of historical method has encouraged his compatriots to run amok, unhampered by any regard for the text of More's *Utopia*, leaving even Professors Oncken and Ritter far behind.

In a review of the latter's work Prof. E. R. Huber does not hesitate to state that it does not make the slightest difference what sort of man More was, the only thing that matters being the »objective content› of his work, the definition of which, however, can only be given in his own words: »Es geht nicht hier um die Frage, ob Morus persönlich eine 'skrupulöse, überzarte und in sich selbst zurückgezogene Persönlichkeit' war ([Ritter] S. 55), ein frommer Mann zudem, der für seine religiöse Überzeugung den Tod auf dem Schafott fand. Entscheidend ist allein der objektive Gehalt seines Werkes, dessen Kern eben darin besteht, dass die Idee des Rechtes benutzt wird, um Unrecht, Gewalttat, Raub und Ausbeutung nicht etwa nur zu verbergen, sondern gerade als höchste und reinste Gerechtigkeit auszugeben. Wenn es irgendwo Machiavellismus in vollendeter Gestalt gab, so nicht im Werk des Machiavell, der in einer fast biederen Weise die Arcana des politischen Machtkampfes preisgab, sondern in diesem Urbild des insularen Cant, wo unter der Maske des machtverneinenden Gerechtigkeitsideals die Methoden, die zu einer umfassenden Weltherrschaft führen sollten, entwickelt wurden. Es sind die Arcana des englischen Imperialismus, die in der 'Utopia' des Morus zuerst niedergelegt worden sind.« (Zeitschrift für die gesamte Staatswissenschaft, vol. 102, Heft 1, 1941, p. 173.)

John Morley wisely remarked that even Machiavelli did not call evil good and good evil, though a past master of violence and fraud like Napoleon might do so (*Machiavelli*, The Romanes Lecture 1897, p. 41). German historians, labouring under a totalitarian regime, have excelled their master even as far as the Third Reich has surpassed the boldest dreams of Machiavelli (cf. Ritter, op. cit. p. 142), and the »objektive Gehalt« of their own ideology, being in itself sufficient justification, is without any regard for the facts of the case applied to heaven and hell with equal facility.

² More's Prefatory Letter to Peter Giles, Lupton, p. 7.
³ Ibid. pp. 7—8 and n. p. 7.
⁴ Letter from Peter Giles to Busleyden, Lupton, pp. xcviii—xcix.

94

⁵ Ritter, op. cit. V. the present writer's review, *Machiavellistisk historie-skrivning*, Svenska Dagbladet, 4 Ap. 1942. Hermann Oncken has fallen a victim to the same temptation. Without venturing on a refutation Prof. Ritter refers to my review in later editions of his book, but so inexactly that I doubt whether he has seen it himself. (*Machtstaat und Utopie*, 3rd and 4th ed., 1943, p. 175.)

Page 26.

¹ John Morley, op. cit., p. 18.

² Lupton, p. 118. It is not impossible that More may have had Xerxes' enterprise in mind, as Brockhaus thinks (op. cit. p. 33), but from this it is a far cry to the rest of his legend of Mount Athos.

³ Lupton, p. 132.

⁴ *Laws*, 797 D—798 D.

⁵ Lupton, e. g. pp. 112—13, 132—3, and 149.

⁶ Viktor Rydberg, *Vapensmeden*, Stockholm, Bonnier, 1891, pp. 150—54. Cf. however Lupton, pp. 137 and 307.

Page 27.

¹ Lupton, p. 122. Prof. Friedrich Brie in *Thomas More der Heitere* (Englische Studien 71, 1936, pp. 46—51) gives a list of humorous details in the *Utopia*.

² Lupton, p. 27.

³ *Cosmographiae Introductio*, pp. 91 sq. and 99. Cf. Lupton, p. 30.

⁴ *Cosmographiae Introductio*, p. 98.

⁵ Ibid. p. 94.   ⁶ Ibid. p. 95.   ⁷ Ibid. pp. 97—8.

⁸ Ibid. pp. 96—8.   ⁹ Ibid. p. 99.   ¹⁰ Ibid. p. 94.

¹¹ Ibid. p. 93.   ¹² Ibid. p. 113.

Page 28.

¹ *De orbe novo. Les huit decades traduites du latin*, Paris 1907, p. 30.

² Ibid. pp. 54—5.

³ *Goda vildar och ädla rövare*, Helsingfors 1941, p. 222.

Page 29.

¹ V. spec. Churton Collins, p. xxxvii and Notes.

² Erasmus to Hutten, Allen, IV, No. 999, p. 21. For the relationship between Plato and More, v. Lina Beeger, *Thomas Morus und Plato. I. Ein Überblick über den platonischen Humanismus*, Tübingen 1879.

³ Lupton, pp. 183 and 230.

⁴ Ibid. pp. 229 and 230—1. It is notable that also among the Polylerites, whose example is quoted by Hythloday in the first book, the serfs or condemned criminals (*sic enim damnatos vocant*, Lupton, p. 68) are set free on fulfilling the same conditions as in Utopia (ibid. p. 70 sq.).

⁵ P. 148.

⁶ Pp. 141 and 183.

[7] Pp. 141—2 and 168.

[8] Pp. 141, 142, 145 and 151 sq. Presumably the number of hours was fixed at six, as being roughly half the amount expected from a European labourer.

[9] Pp. 145—7.

Page 30.

[1] Pp. 147—8.   [2] Pp. 121 and 139.

[3] Pp. 121, 125, 145 and 211.   [4] P. 170.

[5] Pp. 139—41.   [6] P. 280.

Page 31.

[1] Pp. 221—2. Cf. also Plato, *Laws*, 762 D and 942; and More's *Apology*, p. 53.

[2] Hermann Oncken, Introduction, p. 30; A. H. Behrens, whose work has not been accessible to me, quoted ibid., p. 37; Ottmar Dietrich, *Geschichte der Ethik*, Leipzig 1926, III, p. 374 (I owe this reference to the kindness of Prof. K. Rob. V. Wikman). Prof. Kurt Sternberg also has found the institution of serfdom irreconcilable with Utopian socialism (*Über die Utopia des Thomas Morus*, Archiv für Rechts- und Wirtschaftsphilosophie, 26, 1932—3, p. 495). Dr. Michael Freund has taken it even more seriously, making it the very basis of Utopian society and confusing the precautions taken by the Polylerites against any possibility of a rebellion on the part of the serfs with the Utopian constitution which contains no such precautions, the number of serfs being so small (op. cit. pp. 267—9).

Dr. Oswald Bendemann, however, in his *Studie zur Staats- und Socialauffassung des Thomas Morus*, Diss., Berlin 1928, has recognized that »serf» in Utopia is but another name for a felon condemned to hard labour (p. 47). In an excellent manner he refutes Prof. Oncken's presentation of the Utopian »Herrschaftsstaat» (pp. 38—41), analyses the Utopian institution of serfdom (pp. 42—54), and refutes Prof. Oncken's presentation of it (pp. 54—6).

[3] Lupton, pp. 121 and 230.

[4] Ibid. pp. 140 and 150—1.

[5] P. 234.

[6] Pp. 177, 195—9 and 232.

[7] Pp. 130, 132—4 and 149.

[8] Pp. 131 and 143.

Page 32.

[1] P. 152. Cf. pp. 143 and 183.

[2] Pp. 143, 166, 295—6; 184 and 186. More's contempt for astrology was shared by other humanists, v. e. g. Pico's *Adversus astrologos libri XII* and Budé's *De contemptu rerum fortuitarum libri tres*.

[3] Lupton, pp. 184—7 and notes.

[4] Ibid. pp. 174—7.

[5] V. supra p. 2.

[6] Lupton, pp. 177—81.

Page 33.

[1] Roper, p. 6.

[2] Op. cit. pp. 97 and 99.

[3] Lupton, p. 227.

[4] Ibid. pp. 225—6.

[5] Yet M. Dudok may be right in thinking the Utopian custom was devised as a means to prevent the spreading of the »morbus gallicus» or »mal de Naples» which had made its appearance among the armies besieging Naples in 1494 and with the returning French and Spanish troops quickly spread over Europe. (Gerard Dudok, *Sir Thomas More and his Utopia*, Amsterdam [1923], pp. 137—8.) His theory receives some support from the fact that Sir Francis Bacon, although making the inhabitants of his New Atlantis disapprove of it, »for they think it a scorn to give a refusal after so familiar knowledge», yet did no more than modify the Utopian custom in allowing the inspection to be made by a friend of the boy or the girl respectively, while separately bathing in Adam's and Eve's pool. The whole thing, however, may be a fancy inspired by a suggestion in Plato's *Laws*, where the judge decides the time of marriage after inspecting the bridegroom naked and the bride naked to the waist (*Laws*, 925).

Page 34.

[1] Lupton, pp. 224 sq. and 229.

[2] Ibid. pp. 227—9.

[3] The phrase is P. S. Allen's (*Erasmus; Lectures and Wayfaring Sketches*, Oxford, Clarendon Press, 1934, p. 129).

[4] Lupton, pp. 156 and 230.

[5] Ibid. pp. 159—60; and Hallett p. 122 n.

[6] Lupton, pp. 223—4.

Page 35.

[1] Harpsfield, p. 93.

[2] *Republic*, V, iii; *Laws*, IV, 740.

[3] Lupton. pp. 153—6

Page 36.

[1] *Il principe*, Chap. III.

[2] Lupton, pp. 130, 133, 149 and 158.

[3] Ibid. pp. 156 and 161.

[4] Pp. 161—6.

Page 37.

[1] *The History of Utopian Thought*, p. 138.

[2] Lupton, pp. 136 and 231. It is significant that the same rule is applied also in the state of the Polylerites, described in the first book of *Utopia* (Lupton, p. 68).

[3] Ibid. pp. 135—8.

⁴ P. 137. Cf. Caesar, *De bello gallico*, VI, 20; and similar prohibitions in Plato.

Page 38.

¹ Lupton, pp. 234 and 235. Prof. S. B. Liljegren, in support of the similar view held by Harrington, adduces also the opinions of Winstanley, Bacon, Grotius, and Hobbes (*James Harrington's Oceana*, Lund 1924, p. 262).

² Lupton, p. 233.

³ *De civitate Dei*, XIX, 14 ad finem.

⁴ Lupton, pp. 188, 193—4, 202 and 206.

⁵ Ibid. pp. 190, 192 and 194.

⁶ P. 166.

⁷ Pp. 200—201.

⁸ P. 193.

Page 39.

¹ Pp. 170—2. For the reciprocity demanded by this rule, however, cf. supra p. 35.

² E. g. Ritter, op. cit., p. 77, and Freund, op. cit. pp. 271—2 and 275. The latter speaks of the unheard-of novelty of the Utopian financial policy. Yet the arrangement rather resembles that of Plato's Magnesian colony where the citizens must possess neither gold, silver, nor Hellenic coin, but where the state keeps a store of such coin with which it meets the expenses of foreign embassies and expeditions and visits to foreign countries (*Laws*, 742). The German scholars are here playing the part of the Vicar of Croydon, mistaking Utopia for an actually existing state. Like Machiavelli they interpret her intentions according to their own lights.

Page 40.

¹ Lupton, pp. 172—3.

² V. Ritter, op. cit., p. 163: »Wollte Morus seine eigene Idealwelt persiflieren?» Cf. p. 192; and Freund, l. c.: »Aber man arbeitet kaum finanzpolitische Pläne von unerhörter Neuheit aus, wenn sie nichts bedeuten sollen».

³ Lupton, p. 250. Cf. also pp. 238—9.

Page 41.

¹ Ibid. p. 243.

² P. 120.

³ P. 240.

⁴ Lupton, p. 238. I have altered Robynson's »great byshopes» to »popes» (summorum pontificum).

⁵ Frederic Seebohm, *The Oxford Reformers*, London, Longmans Green & Co., 2nd ed. 1869, p. 265.

Page 42.

¹ Lupton, pp. 241—2.

² Ibid. p. 307.

98

³ Pp. 116—8 and 129.
⁴ Pp. 123 and 243.
⁵ Pp. 243—4.

Page 43.
¹ Pp. 233—42. Cf. H. Dietzel, op. cit. p. 376; Bendemann, op. cit. pp. 72—3; and F. Brie, *Machtpolitik und Krieg in der Utopia des Thomas More*, Historisches Jahrbuch 61, 1941, p. 131: »Es handelt sich in keinem Falle um Erweiterung von Macht, Gewinn an Gütern oder Erwerb von Kriegsruhm, sondern immer nur um die Wiederherstellung von verletztem Recht, des eigenen oder des der Freunde, mit anderen Worten um Krieg als Akt der Gerechtigkeit». Prof. Hermann Oncken, however, in a subtle piece of reasoning, repeated with less conviction by Gerhard Ritter, argues that an ideal society can only exist in isolation and that More's philanthropic programme breaks down the moment his ideal commonwealth is brought into contact with other countries (Introduction, p. 31; Heidelberger Akademie, p. 17). Dr. Oswald Bendemann, however, in an excellent argument based on the text of *Utopia*, has convincingiy disproved Oncken's theory of an *Ur-Utopia*, conceived in complete isolation (op. cit. pp. 26—32). From a philosophical point of view Oncken's arguments have been refuted by Prof. K. Sternberg (*Über die Utopia des Thomas Morus*, Archiv für Rechts- und Wirtschaftsphilosophie 27, 1933—4, pp. 249—55). With more originality than common sense Prof. E. R. Huber, on the contrary, criticizes Oncken because he has overlooked the fact that only the exploitation of other countries enables the Utopians to realise their own social ideals: »humanitäre Ideologie und brutale Gewaltpolitik stehen in einem untrennbaren Zusammenhang; nur weil die Utopier eine bis in die letzten konsequenzen entwickelte humanitäre Ideologie besitzen, können sie die ihnen specifische Art von Machtpolitik entwickeln; nur diese rücksichtslose Machtpolitik aber setzt sie in den Stand, in weitem Umfange, vor allem in der Innenpolitik, ihrem humanitären Programm zu folgen» (op. cit. p. 172). Such reasoning may have some connexion with the critic's own ideas concerning the aims of the Third Reich; it certainly has nothing whatever to do with *Utopia*.

Utopia is not an ideal republic in that sense. Utopian citizens commit crimes and suffer grievous punishment just in the same way as in the field of international affairs aggressors commit wrongs and are punished with cruel warfare. Hence Oncken's elaborate reconstruction of the composition of *Utopia* is mistaken at this point. There is no need to suppose those parts to be later additions which treat of Utopian relations with other countries, for they rest on the same suppositions as the relations of the Utopians among themselves (v. infra). Neither was More the first to make his imaginary republic defend itself and the order for which it stands against attacks from outside. Elaborate preparations for war characterize both the *Republic* and the *Laws* of Plato, though More has spread his vision farther. It is worth while looking at some of Oncken's arguments a little more closely. Talking of the reasons for which the Utopians go to war, he says: »Drittens kennt man auch einen Befreiungskrieg zu gunsten eines 'von Tyrannen unterdrückten Volkes'. Da es augenscheinlich die utopische, also kommunistische Denkweise ist, die über den Begriff des Tyrannen und der Unterdrückung entscheidet, so könnte damit jeder Propagandakrieg gerechtfertigt werden; und wenn wir uns für einen Augenblick entschliessen, Utopien zu verlassen und in die Geschichte hinüberzutreten, so müssten wir bekennen, dass alle Arten der Interventionstheorie, seien sie nun reaktionär oder revolutionär begründet, und nicht minder alle Arten der zivilisatorisch oder ähnlich verkleideten Eroberungsmethoden mit dem bedenklichen Grundsatz der Utopier sehr zufrieden sein könnten.« (Heidelberger Akademie, p. 15.) Professor Oncken has forgotten that the Utopians do not conquer territory at all and that their friends have »their owne priuate gooddes« (Lupton, p. 246). But no historian worthy of the name can be ignorant of what More means by the »Tyranni iugo et servitute« from which the Utopians liberate nations by force of arms, for from Isocrates and down the centuries classical and mediæval writers have defined a King as a ruler over free men, but a Tyrant as a ruler over slaves. St. Augustine, for whom More entertained such a special reverence, said that »if justice is set aside, what are kingdoms but robberies on a large scale?« (*De civitate Dei*, IV, 4.) With mediæval writers on statecraft, like Isidore of Seville, John of Salisbury, Dante, and Pierre Dubois, the prince who breaks the law becomes a tyrant according to the classical pattern. Does not More call him a jailor (carceris custodem, Lupton, p. 94)? John of Salisbury is even less complimentary, describing him as »the image of crooked Lucifer« (luciveranae pravitatis imago). — So far from fighting in order to impose communism on others the Utopians actually go to war in order to defend the private property of the citizens of other states (Lupton, p. 246). It is, once more, in defence of law and order that the Utopians take up their arms, neither for intervention, nor expansion. A less prejudiced German critic has recognized in More's *Richard III* a »Vorstudie« to the *Utopia* inasmuch as in this work More places the »good king«, Edward IV, in a position of contrast with the »tyrant«, Richard III (H. Glunz, *Shakespeare und Morus*, Kölner anglistische Arbeiten, 1938, pp. 26—9), but then of course Gerhard Ritter would object to the habit of quoting one book in support of another (op. cit. p. 164).

But Oncken goes on: »Schliesslich fehlt auch der Handelskrieg nicht, zwar nicht für die eigenen Interessen der Utopier, die von ihrer Wirtschaftsform aus gar keinen Handel treiben [an odd statement to make], aber doch für die Interessen ihrer Freunde, falls deren Kaufleute irgendwo in einem fremden Lande in ihren Rechten verkürzt werden sollten. Nehmen wir zu dem allen noch den schon erwähnten Kolonialkrieg zum Erwerb benötigten Siedlungslandes hinzu, so erhalten wir eine stattliche Liste von Fictionen zur Begründung des seit Augustinus immer wieder erörterten bellum justum. Diese utopische Kasuistik, die über die Sätze der mittelalterlichen Kanonisten weit hinausreicht, vermag auch die anspruchsvollste Theorie des

Krieges zu befriedigen. Sie erscheint noch bedenklicher als die Machtlehre Machiavells, weil alle moralisierende Kasuistik einen unmoralischen Kern in sich schliesst. Die englische Geschichte lehrt, dass gerade in diesem Volke das Bedürfnis nach einer ethisch formulierten Rechtfertigung eines Krieges zu allen Zeiten sehr lebendig ist.» (Ibid. pp. 15—16.)

Again Prof. Oncken has overlooked the fact that the Utopians derive no advantage from what he calls the »Handelskrieg» (Lupton, pp. 244—5). On the contrary, they regard war as »too cruel an act to revenge that loss [of money] with the death of many» (p. 246). It has been declared in the first book to be »no right nor justice that the loss of money should cause the loss of man's life» (p. 60). To the question of the colonial wars, which are more in the nature of the quelling of a rebellion, I shall return presently (v. infra pp. 60—65). What matters in this place is the motive that moves the peace-loving Utopians to go to war in the two instances here mentioned, and again it is no other than the defence of law and order against criminal action. The Utopians are not committed to go to the assistance of their friends unconditionally in this instance, and »this they do not, unless their counsel and advice in the matter be asked, whiles it is yet new and fresh. For if they find the cause probable [i. e. proved, probata causa], and if the contrary part will not restore again such things as be of them justly demanded, then they be the chief authors and makers of the war» (Lupton, p. 244). So far from seeking hypocritical pretexts for war, the Utopians on the contrary do everything they can to avoid it, unless justice requires it. Prof. Oncken's reference to English history is consequently more flattering than he intended. The question of Utopian and Machiavellian morals I have dealt with elsewhere. (V. *Historisk demonologi* and *Machiavellistisk historieskrivning.*)

Seeing how wide of the mark are the arguments of Prof. Oncken, a detailed refutation of his views would have been superfluous, if they had not come to be regarded as Gospel-truth in Germany. His influence became apparent as early as 1924 in Friedrich Meinecke's *Die Idee der Staatsräson* (2nd ed., 1925, p. 491); in Ottmar Dietrich's *Geschichte der Ethik*, 1926 (III, p. 374); and though, under the influence of R. W. Chambers, he has since made honourable amends (Historisches Jahrbuch, 1941, p. 116 n. 2), even Prof. Friedrich Brie fell a victim to Oncken's suggestions in *Deismus und Atheismus in der englischen Renaissance* (Anglia 48, 1924, pp. 76 sq., 91, and 164) and in the second edition of *Imperialistische Strömungen in der englischen Literatur*, 1928 (p. 16 sqq.). The able refutations by Karl Vorländer, Oswald Bendemann, and K. Sternberg have received scant iustice at the hands of later German critics, and the influence of Oncken remains predominant in the contributions of i. a. Messrs. Freund, Ritter, and Huber. The reviews of Ritter's *Machtstaat und Utopie* reflect the obsession (v. e. g. E. R. Huber, op. cit.; Herman Gummerus, Finsk Tidskrift cxxix, April 1941; and Karl Brandi, Vergangenheit und Gegenwart xxxii, 1942, pp. 247—8). It has even conquered the presidential chair of the Prussian Academy of Sciences. (Prof. Theodor Vahlen, *Ansprache des*

Präsidenten, Öffentliche Festsitzung zur Feier des Friedrichstages und des Tages der Reichsgründung, 23 Jan. 1941; and *Ansprache des Präsidenten* on the same occasion 1942, Jahrbuch der Preussischen Akademie der Wissenschaften 1941, p. 148, and 1942 pp. 113—19. I owe the reference to the courtesy of Prof. Eilert Ekwall.)

In the later editions of his book Prof. Ritter, it is true, confesses a change of heart with regard to the *Utopia*. Whereas in 1922 he very largely subscribed to the theses of Hermann Oncken, he has since modified his views (3rd and 4th ed. p. 190). Yet many traces of Oncken's influence remain (e. g. pp. 76—7, 79—80, 83, 87—8 and 91—2), notably in his ill-advised polemic against Prof. Friedrich Brie (pp. 190—4), which betrays a startling lack of any deeper understanding either of More or of his work. Nor can I regard his professed change of heart as sincere while he insists on attributing to St. Thomas More »jene Neigung zu moralischer Schönfärberei und Verbrämung der Machtpolitik, die wir den englischen cant nennen» (p. 191; cf. also p. 181).

The Utopian criticism in Germany thus provides striking illustrations of the degradation of scholarship intent on serving a transient ideology. (Cf. J. Huizinga, *Im Bann der Geschichte*, pp. 58 and 86—93; and the review by Prof. Ragnar Josephson, *Historisk Skepsis*, Svenska Dagbladet 13 Nov. 1943.)

² Harpsfield, pp. 177, 193 sq. and 196.

³ Lupton, pp. 245 and 248.

⁴ Ibid. pp. 247 and 248.

Page 44.

¹ Pp. 248—51 and notes. Cf. also Churton Collins, notes pp. 230 and 231.

² Yet Prof. Oncken says (Heidelberger Akademie, p. 16): »Geht man zu der Kriegsführung der Utopier über, so gibt es vollends kein Halten mehr; sie ist grundsätzlich ebenso hart wie diejenige anderer Völker. . . Bei Kriegsbeginn schreiben die Utopier hohe Belohnungen für die Ermordung der feindlichen Fürsten und ihrer Ratgeber aus, und verdoppeln sie, wenn sie lebendig eingebracht werden; historische Belege aus den Niederungen der englischen Publicistik und Praxis dafür beizubringen, will ich mir versagen.» There is no need. The only historical argument is the practice of Henry VIII and his contemporaries, and that is exactly what More is attacking with his biting satire. Karl Kautsky wisely recognized this (op. cit. 3rd. ed., Stuttgart 1913, p. 301). Werner Sombart also was more cautious, for though he reduces the Utopian benevolence towards other nations to »cant», he recognizes that: »Man weiss bei Morus nie, wo sein Ernst aufhört und sein Spott anfängt. Deshalb kann dieses Ideal von der Kriegsführung ebensowohl eine Verhöhnung der Krämer bedeuten, die der grosse Kanzler damals unter seinen Landsleuten emporkommen und an Einfluss gewinnen sah.» (*Händler und Helden, Patriotische Besinnungen*, Munich and Leipzig 1915, p. 33. I owe the reference to the kindness of Dr. C. O. von Feilitzen.) Cf. however also Plato's *Republic*, where wars against other Greeks are humanely

fought, because the citizens recognize that only a few are their foes, namely those who are to blame for the quarrel. Hence they carry the war only to the point of compelling the guilty to fulfill the demands of justice. (*Republic*, V, xvi.) The Utopians, we are told, in matters of philosophy and logic »be almost equal to our old ancient clerks» (Lupton, p. 184).

[3] Lupton, pp. 47—51. More objects to mercenaries because they are one of the causes of wars and at best a nuisance in peace. Machiavelli characteristically disapproves of them because they are bad soldiers. His portrait of them is not much more flattering than More's (*Principe*, XII). Dr. Michael Freund, however, makes the mercenaries the very backbone of the Utopian defence system (op. cit. pp. 261, 263 n, 265 n, 272—3, and 274 n). It becomes to him an absolute Utopian ideal, realised thanks to their ingenious capitalist system (p. 271).

Page 45.

[1] Lupton, pp. 252—4 and notes.
[2] Ibid. pp. 254—5.
[3] Pp. 255 and 265.

Page 46.

[1] P. 256.
[2] *Republic*, V, xiv and xvii. Prof. K. Sternberg reminds us also that Phaedrus in the Symposium pronounces the opinion that an army consisting of none but lovers would, in spite of their small numbers, be victorious in battle against practically the whole world (Archiv für Rechts- und Wirtschaftsphilosophie 26, p. 487). Cf. also Lupton, p. 257 n., who points to parallels to the Utopian custom in Caesar and Tacitus.
[3] Lupton, p. 257.

Page 47.

[1] Ibid. pp. 258—62.
[2] Pp. 259 and 263—4.

Page 48.

[1] P. 265.
[2] Sir John Fortescue, op. cit., pp. 115 and 138. That the same held good even a hundred years later is proved by Sir Walter Ralegh's reflections on the advantages of sea power in his *History of the World* and by Francis Bacon's argument that the key to political greatness is to be found »in the commandment of the sea» (*On the true Greatness of Great Britain*). Dr. Oswald Bendemann rightly emphasizes the fact that when the *Utopia* was written England, so far from being invulnerable to foreign aggression, was on the contrary exposed to the double threat of invasion both from France and from Scotland (op. cit. pp. 35—6). The battle of Flodden had been fought barely three years before.

Nor is the relative isolation of Utopia a necessary consequence of its being an »ideal» republic, as Oncken thought, but an integral part of the author's make-believe, for if it were represented as existing in lively communication with the known world, it could have been »no news» to the reader. (Cf. the inaccessible situation of the country of the Polylerites in the first book, a feature deriving from the mediæval legends of an earthly paradise.)

³ Oncken, Introduction, p. 39; Heidelberger Akademie, pp. 22—5; Ritter, op. cit., pp. 74 and 100. That Utopia is to be identified with England »versteht sich von selbst» (Ritter, p. 74). Freund (op. cit. pp. 254 and 261—2) is a little more cautious. But with the recognition of the exposed position of England another theory of the German casuists is overthrown, namely that Germany, as being hemmed in by neighbours, must of necessity be reduced to a Machiavellian policy (Oncken, Introduction, p. 39; Heidelberger Akademie, l. c.; Ritter, more cryptically, pp. 92—8).

Page 49.

¹ Lupton, pp. 236—7.
² Sir John Harington's phrase about More himself.
³ Ritter, op. cit., p. 80; Oncken as follows: »Man fühlt sich an römischen Prokonsuln in unterworfenen Provinzen erinnert, ja von ferne, als wenn das Auge des Morus solches prophetisch hätte voraussehen können, scheinen die Umrisse einer Herrschaftsstellung aufzutauchen, wie England sie seine Söhne in den nächsten Jahrhunderten in allen Erdteilen ausüben lassen konnte. So weit ist das Denken des Morus über seinen Ausgangspunkt hinausgetrieben worden. Der kommunistische und primitiv-agrarische Idealstaat, der sich bereits in der Sklavenfrage als Klassenstaat enthüllte, stellt sich nunmehr als ein machtpolitischer Herrschaftsstaat mit Ansätzen zu einem fast modern-anmutenden kapitalistischen Imperialismus dar» (Introduction, p. 37). And further; »So weit hat sich der Idealist Morus von seinen Ausgangspunkten ... abtreiben lassen ... Die Erklärung liegt darin, dass durch alle utopische Vorsichtsmassregeln der Staatsisolierung ein tiefer englischer Instinkt hemmungslos durchbricht, sobald die Isolierung als aufgehoben gedacht wird. Dieser Instinkt verwirft wohl eine kontinentale Eroberungspolitik nach Art Heinrichs VIII., weil sie ihm falsch und überlebt erscheint, nicht aber eine Richtung der Machtpolitik, die dem Genius der Nation entsprechend ist. Auf ihren Wegen vermag sich auch Morus mit dem Wesen der Macht zu versöhnen. So zeichnet er die Umrisse einer kolonialen und maritimen Machtausweitung: Siedelung über See, nationales Merkantilsystem, Bündnissmaschinerie, Vasallengefolge, wenn man will die Ansätze einer kapitalitischen Weltausbeutung. Es ist als ob die Phantasie vor vierhundert Jahren schon die moderne Herrschaftsstellung der Angelsachsen in der Welt zu ahnen vermöchte» (Heidelberger Akademie, p. 17). If the British Commonwealth and Empire is so faithfully anticipated in Utopia, never has it received a better testimonial.

When sending the Utopian magistrates abroad, however, More in fact expresses a humanist ideal, as Dr. Bendemann has pointed out (op. cit. p. 76). The model is Plato's Athenian Academy where young men were educated to serve as administrators and counsellors to rulers of states to whose dominions they were invited.

⁴ Lupton, pp. 266—7.

Page 50.

¹ Ibid. pp. 267—9 and notes.

² Pp. 271—4. Cf. also pp. 269—71.

³ Pp. 274—6. It should not be forgotten that unbelief had reached such proportions in Europe that Pope Leo X in 1513 considered it necessary to cause the Lateran Council to confirm by statute the doctrine of the immortality and individuality of the soul. No later than 1516, however, in the year of *Utopia* and only a few days after its publication, appeared Pomponazzi's famous book *De immortalitate animae* in which the impossibility of any philosophical proof of immortality was upheld.

Page 51.

¹ Lupton, pp. 276—9.

² Ibid. pp. 279—82.

³ Mgr. Hallett's note in his edition of *Utopia*, p. 208. Cf. *English Works*, Campbell, II, p. 225 C.

Page 52.

¹ Lupton, pp. 282—3 and 286—7. In Europe the immunity of the clergy was under debate.

² Ibid. pp. 284—5.

³ Pp. 285—6.

⁴ Pp. 287—9.

Page 54.

¹ Pp. 289—98.

² Pp. 298 and 308—9.

Page 55.

¹ More's Prefatory Letter to Peter Giles, Lupton, p. 1; More to Erasmus, 3 Sept. 1516, Allen, II, No. 461, p. 339; Erasmus to Hutten, Allen, IV, No. 999, p. 21.

² Oncken, Introduction, pp. 33—40; Heidelberger Akademie, pp. 10—19. Cf. supra pp. 43 n. 1; 44 n. 2; 48 n. 3; and 49 n. 3.

Page 56.

¹ E. g. Roper, p. 24; More to Wolsey, Delcourt, p. 324, *Letters and Papers*, III, ii, p. 1085.

² Lupton, pp. 239—41, 248—9, 251 and 252—5.

[3] Ibid. pp. 173, 238—9 and 250.

[4] Sir James Mackintosh, *Sir Thomas More*, 1831, p. 61.

[5] Ritter, op. cit., p. 72. Cf. also Michael Freund (op. cit.) and E. R. Huber (op. cit.). Prof. Kurt Sternberg also has found an abyss between Utopian war aims and means (Archiv für Rechts- und Wirtschaftsphiloso-phie 26, p. 478). Georg Ellinger as long ago as 1887 reduced this supposed inconsistency to the general standard of Mediæval and Renaissance morals (*Thomas Morus und Machiavelli* in Vierteljahrschrift für Kultur und Literatur der Renaissanse, II, 1887, pp. 17—26. V. spec. pp. 21—22). It is, however, worth noting that at the end of the dialogue More in his own person disclaims »many things», i. a. »in the fassion of their cheualry». (Lupton, p. 307.)

Page 57.

[1] Lupton, p. 122. V. supra p. 26 sq.

[2] Ibid. p. 176; supra p. 32; Oncken, l. c. Yet Hythloday himself points to the example of the ancient Romans (Lupton, p. 64). Georg Ellinger (op. cit. p. 20) has found a model in Herodotus.

[3] Lupton, p. 175.

[4] Ibid. p. 181. Supra p. 32 sq. Georg Ellinger (op. cit. p. 20) points to Lucian's *Nigrinus* as the source of this incident.

[5] Pp. 51—8.

Page 58.

[1] P. 92.

[2] Roper, pp. 12—16.

[3] Lupton, pp. 81—7. Cf. supra p. 56 n. 1.

Page 59.

[1] Ibid. p. 269.

[2] Pp. 112 and 184. Cf. Stapleton, pp. 40—2.

[3] Lupton, pp. 141 and 168. Cf. Erasmus' description of More's house-hold in Letter to Budé, Allen IV, No. 1233, p. 577.

[4] V. supra pp. 30 sq. and 31 n. 1.

[5] Lupton, v. spec. pp. 144 sq. and 199. Cf. Erasmus to Hutten, Allen, IV, No. 999, p. 16.

[6] Lupton, p. 165; Stapleton, p. 97.

Page 60.

[1] Lupton, pp. 164 and 231 sq. Cf. Erasmus, l. c., and Roper, pp. 43—4.

[2] Lupton, pp. 210—11; Roper, p. 49.

Page 61.

[1] Introduction, p. 34; Heidelberger Akademie, p. 14 sq.

[2] Heidelberger Akademie, p. 17.

[3] R. W. Chambers, op. cit., pp. 139—43.

Page 62.

[1] Ibid. p. 141.

[2] Lupton, pp. 154—6. It is notable that the motivation is the same as that given by the Utopians when they do not ask for payment of foreign debts unless they need them. »For that thing which is to them no profit, to take it from other to whom it is profitable, they think it no right nor conscience› (p. 172). — I note with satisfaction that Prof. Friedrich Brie has drawn attention to this parallel in his excellent review of Ritter's *Machtstaat und Utopie* (Hist. Jahrbuch 1941, p. 127). — It is worth noting also that there is no suggestion of employing mercenaries or in fact foreign troops of any kind in colonial warfare, as A. H. Behrens pretends in his characterization of *Utopia* as »eine Gesellschaft, gegründet auf Sklaverei und erweitert durch Kriege, die mit geworbenen Söldnern geführt werden» (quot. Oncken, Introduction, p. 37). The colonial wars are the only ones that lead to any expansion of territory.

Page 64.

[1] Ritter, op. cit., p. 164.

[2] Pace Ritter, ibid. p. 86. Although Dr. Michael Freund has recognized that More suggested colonization as a palliative against what he calls the »Bevölkerungsdruck», yet he insists on its forming part of the Utopian system of power politics and so attributes to the *Utopia* a double nature of philanthropy where Utopian citizens are concerned and ruthless imperialism in the colonial sphere (op. cit. pp. 256 und 265). Whereas Dr. Bendemann ably refutes Oncken's statements on the subject of Utopian colonization (op. cit. pp. 32—5), Friedrich Brie has emphatically contradicted Ritter's thesis of Utopian superiority over other races: ›Der Krieg, den die Utopier gegen andere Völker führen, ist niemals der von Hellenen gegen Barbaren mit dem Ziel der völligen Unterjochung bis zur Sklaverei oder Ausrottung, sondern deutlich der von Hellenen gegen Hellenen ohne Verheerung des Landes und ohne Vorgehen gegen die Einwohner. Während Plato im Überlegenheitsgefühl des Griechen bestimmt, dass kein Hellene einen Hellenen zum Sklaven haben soll, lässt More auch die Utopier zu Sklaven degradiert werden.» (Hist. Jahrbuch 1941, p. 137). The distinction was noticed by Kautsky (op. cit. p. 301).

Page 65.

[1] Pace Ritter, p. 80.

Page 67.

[1] *A Dialogue of Comfort against Tribulation*, ed. Mgr. P. E. Hallett, Burns Oates & Washbourne, 1937, pp. 169—70.

[2] Tyndale's *Answer to Sir Thomas More's Dialogue*, ed. H. Walter, Parker Society, Cambridge 1850, p. 16.

[3] *English Works*, 1557, p. 422; quoted A. I. Taft, *Apology of Sir Thomas More*, pp. vii—viii.

Page 68.

[1] *English Works*, pp. 422—3; quoted Hallett, *Utopia*, pp. 64—5 n.
[2] *Apology*, p. 86. I have modernized the spelling and punctuation.
[3] Ibid. pp. 93—4.

Page 69.

[1] Lupton, p. 109.   [2] Ibid. p. 101.
[3] P. 105.   [4] P. 106 sq.

Page 70.

[1] P. 104 sq. The conclusion of Johannes Kühn (*Thomas Morus und Rousseau*, Historische Vierteljahrschrift, XXIII, Dresden 1926, pp. 161—87) that More had given bad institutions the blame for man being evil is not justified even from Hythloday's argument. It is one thing to say that »possessions be private» and another »that money beareth all the stroke». It is part of More's *jeu d'esprit* to trick us into identifying the two. He makes Hythloday attack the institution while he is actually attacking its perversion.
[2] *Apology*, pp. 86—94. Cf. also *Dialogue of Comfort*, pp. 158—75.
[3] Lupton, pp. 109—10.
[4] Ibid. pp. 307—8.

Page 71.

[1] P. 100.   [2] P. 109.   [3] P. 309.
[4] P. 100.   [5] Ed. Born, p. 143.   [6] *Apology*, p. 189.

Page 72.

[1] *De communione rerum*, 1538; transl. Foster Watson, op. cit., p. cxii sq.
[2] *De Ecclesiae concordia*, 1533; paraphrased P. S. Allen, *Erasmus*; *Lectures and Wayfaring Sketches*, p. 95.
[3] V. supra p. 67 sq.

Page 73.

[1] *Dialogue of Comfort*, pp. 170—1.
[2] Op. cit. passim. V. spec. p. 281.

Page 74.

[1] Lupton, pp. 100—101.
[2] Ibid. p. 34.
[3] See the present writer's *The Interpretation of Utopia*, A Philological Miscellany presented to Eilert Ekwall, Studia Neophilologica, XV, 2, 1942, pp. 43—8.
[4] There is a fundamental truth behind those feelings which have made Heinrich Brockhaus construct his hypothesis, though the details are sheer fantasy. Cf. R. W. Chambers, op. cit., pp. 137—8.

Page 76.

[1] Op. cit p. 127.

[2] Joh. Pici *Oratio de hominis dignitate.*

[3] Lupton, pp. 217—18.

Page 77.

[1] Ibid. p. 187—8.

[2] Hythloday about the law of Moses, Lupton, p. 62.

[3] Ibid. p. 63.

[4] English Works, Campbell, II, p. 152.

[5] *Dialogue of Comfort*, p. 287.

Page 78.

[1] V. spec. Christopher Hollis, op. cit. Cf. also the present writer, *Kristen Humanism*, Huvudstadsbladet, 14 Feb. 1943.

[2] Lupton, p. 101 sq.

[3] Ibid. p. 61. Hythloday himself in suggesting forced labour as a punishment for crimes pointed to the example of the Romans (Lupton, p. 64). Dr. Oswald Bendemann speaks of More's »fast antiquarischer Klassicismus» in the description of the Utopian preparedness for war (op. cit. p. 64).

[4] Born, p. 143.

[5] Ibid. p. 203.

Page 79.

[1] *De tradendis disciplinis*, V, ii, Foster Watson, p. 248 sq.

[2] Lupton, p. 60.

Page 80.

[1] Seebohm in his otherwise excellent and still most valuable book on *The Oxford Reformers* has committed the error of regarding Utopia as More's ultimate ideal. In a penetrating analysis of Utopian thought Prof. Kurt Sternberg also has wrongly identified the Utopian philosophy with More's own (Archiv für Rechts- und Wirtschaftsphilosophie 26, 1932—3, pp. 464—97, and 27, 1933—34, pp. 232—57). The numerous inconsistencies are traced to their origin in the tension between the component parts, such as Platonic and Aristotelian, Epicurean and Stoic elements, idealism and materialism, communism and individualism. The intellectual quality of More's thought thus becomes over-stressed. It is however notable to what extent 18th century philosophy was anticipated in *Utopia*. Yet it is characteristic that in the Utopian idea of mercy, as applied to repentant sinners, Prof. Sternberg has seen a means whereby the various elements of Utopian thought are reconciled and harmoniously merged into a higher unity (p. 480 sq.). It is exactly Christianity with its »new law of clemency and mercy» which gives to More's own philosophy the unity which Prof. Sternberg misses in Utopia. — I regret not having had access to Mr. Robert T.

Adams's article on *The Philosophic Unity of More's Utopia* in Studies in
Philology, Jan. 1941.

² H. Glunz, op. cit., p. 15 n.

³ It would carry us too far to enter on the question of More's own
application of his ideal of toleration. The late R. W. Chambers has con-
clusively shown that neither was he responsible for the persecution and
cruelty of which he has been accused, nor was his practice inconsistent
with the Utopian ideal. (Op. cit. pp. 264—7 and 274—82.) Cf. also the present
writer, *Thomas More och samvetets frihet*, Svenska Dagbladet, 8 Oct. 1942.

⁴ For illustrations of More's attitude, v. *Apology*: »I fynde not yet suche
plenty and store of vertue in my selfe, as to thynke it a metely parte and
conuenyent for me to play, to rebuke as abomynable vycyouse folke, any one
honest companye eyther spyrytuall or temporall & mych lesse mete to rebuke
& reproche eyther the whole spyrytualtye or temporaltye, bycause of suche
as are very starke noughte in bothe.» (Pp. 54—5. Cf. also pp. 58, 98,
and 104.)

⁵ Lupton, p. 237.   ⁶ Cf. Roper, p. 45.

Page 81.

¹ V. *The Month and Catholic Review* 1874, quoted by Dr. Lupton,
p. xxxvi, and the recent works of Mr. Christopher Hollis and Mgr. Hallett.
Mr. Algernon Cecil in his *A Potrait of Thomas More. Scholar, Statesman,
Saint.* Eyre & Spottiswood 1937, and Mr. Daniel Sargent in *Thomas More*,
Sheed & Ward 1936, have adopted it. Among German critics only two
have come to my knowledge, i. e. Professors Friedrich Brie and Hans Glunz.

² Lupton, p. lxxxvii sq. Cf. also the dictum of Beatus Rhenanus concerning
More and his *Utopia*: »Et docet minus forsan philosophice, quam illi
[Plato, Aristoteles et Iustiniani Pandectae], sed magis christiane» (More's
Opera Omnia, Francfort 1689, p. 232).

³ Roper, p. 83.

⁴ Lupton, p. 104.

Page 82.

¹ F. M. Nichols, *Epistles of Erasmus*, II, p. 576.

² Matthew, X, 24. Cf. *English Works* of More, ed. Campbell, I, p. 21;
Dialogue of Comfort, pp. 40, 274 and 292; and Roper, p. 26 sq.

³ Lupton, p. 34.

⁴ *Apology*, p. 58.

⁵ Lupton, p. 95.

⁶ *Apology*, pp. 58—9.

⁷ Ibid. p. 75. Cf. also *Dialogue of Comfort*, p. 175: »Let every man
fear and think in this world, that all the good that he doth, or can do, is
a great deal too little.»

INDEX

A Modern Utopia, of Wells, 4.
A Treatise Concerning the Division between the Spiritualty and Temporalty, see »Pacifyer».
Absurdities, of Utopia, 57, 74, 79, 81.
Abuses, the object of More's criticism, 67, 80, 82, 107, 108.
Achorians, the, 14, 20, 23, 74.
Act of Parliament, on Enclosures, 13.
Adams, Robert T., *Philosophic Unity of More's Utopia,* 108 sq.
Administration, of Utopia, 36—7.
Adultery, 34.
Advice, unwillingness to take, 18, 19, 20; willingness of philosophers to give, 21.
Aegidius, Petrus, *see* Giles, Peter.
Aesop, 67, 74.
Aged, the, reverence for, 34, 60.
Agressors, 42—3, 63—4, 82, 98, 100; defined, 100.
Agriculture, 13, 30, 57.
Ahlberg, Alf, 85.
Aimara Indians, 17.
Alexander the Great, 41.
Alexander VI, Pope, 41.
Allen, P. S. and H. M., *Opus Epistolarum Des. Erasmi Roterodami,* 84, 86, 88, 89, 91, 94, 104, 105; *Selections from More's English Works,* 87, 88, 91; *Erasmus;* — *lectures and wayfaring sketches,* 96, 107; quoted, 34, 72.
Alliances, 41 sq.
Alternation, of town and country life, 30.
Amaurote, »the city of shadows», chief city of Utopia, 32, 36, 60.
Ambassadors, Anemolian, 2, 32—3, 57; European, 1, 2.
Amelioràtion, *Utopia* as stimulus to, 60, 82.
An Englishman Looks at the World, of Wells, 84; quoted, 2.
Anabaptists, the, 72.
Anarchy, 76.
Anemolians, the, 2, 32.
Anglia, 84, 10c.

Annotations to the Pandects, of Budé, 86.
Antiquarianism, of More, 93, 108.
Anyder, »Lackwater», river in Utopia, 4.
Apology, of More, 68, 69, 70, 71, 82, 90, 91, 95, 106, 107, 109; quoted, 68, 71, 109.
Archiv für Rechts- und Wirtschaftsphilosophie, 95, 98, 102, 105, 108.
Aristotle, 13, 29, 109.
Aristotelian element, in *Utopia,* 108.
Arithmetic, 32.
Asceticism, 60, 77.
Astrology, 32.
Astronomy, 32.
Athens, ancient, 31.
Atlantis, 28.
Augustine, St., 33, 38, 49, 72, 81, 92, 99; *De civitate Dei,* 33, 38, 81, 97, 99; More's lecture on, 33.
Authority, of government, 37, 70.

Bacon, Sir Francis, Lord Verulam, 4, 96, 97, 102; *New Atlantis,* 4, 96.
Bagley, Walter, ed. *Nova Solyma,* 85.
Balance, of industries in Utopia, 30.
Bankers, 12.
Barclay, Alexander, 15.
Beeger, Lina, *Morus und Plato,* 94.
Beggary, causes of, 13, 19, 86.
Behrens, A. H., 95, 106.
Bellamy, Edward, 3, 5, 38.
Bellum iustum, 35, 42—3, 46, 62, 63, 98, 99—100.
Bendemann, Oswald, *Staatsauffassung des Thomas Morus,* 95, 98, 100, 102, 104, 106, 108.
Bible, Holy, 9, 90.
Bibliographies, 85.
Birds' feathers, precious in West Indies, 27; in Utopia, 53.
Bloodshed, avoided by the Utopians, 40, 43—4.
Bolshevist view of *Utopia,* 3 sq.
Bonaparte, Napoleon, 93.

Bondage, 29, 30, 31, 34, 47, 78, 79, 95, 108.

Bondmen, 29, 30—1, 35, 38, 79, 94, 95, 106.

Born, L. K., ed. Institutio principis Christiani, 86, 87, 90, 91, 107, 108.

Bourbon, Charles, Duke of, 87.

Brandi, Karl, 100.

Brandt, Sebastian, 15.

Brave New World, of Huxley, 4.

Brewer, J. S., Letters and Papers, 88, 104; Reign of Henry VIII, 88.

Brie, Friedrich, 100, 101, 106, 109; Deismus und Atheismus, 100; Macht-politik und Krieg in Utopia, 98, 100, 106; Thomas More der Heitere, 94.

Brockhaus, Heinrich, 107; Die Utopia-schrift des Thomas Morus, 90, 94.

Buckingham, Henry Stafford, 2nd Duke, 22.

Budé, Guillaume, 3, 6, 12, 81, 86, 87, 95; Annotations to the Pandects, 86; De contemptu rerum fortuitarum, 95; De Asse, 86; L'instruction du prince, 87; letter to Lupset, 84; quoted, 81; letter from Erasmus, 105.

Bulwer-Lytton, Edward Robert, see Lytton, 1st Earl.

Burial, 34, 51.

Busleyden, Hiernone, letter to More, 89; dedication of Utopia, 61; letter from Peter Giles, 93.

Butchers, in Utopia only bondmen, 38.

Butler, Samuel, 5.

Cabet, Etienne, 3.

Cabot, John, 61.

Caesar, Julius, 29, 41, 97, 102; De bello gallico, 97.

Campanella, Thomas, 4.

Campbell, W. E., More's Utopia and his Social Teaching, 85; ed. English Works of More, 88, 89, 91, 104, 107, 109.

Capital punishment, 3; in Europe, 12 sq., 79, 87; in Utopia, 3, 31, 34, 47, 79; argument against, 12 sq.

Capitalist system, 11, 12, 59; see also property, private.

Catherine, of Aragon, 2.

Catholic view of Utopia, 81.

Cecil, Algernon, Thomas More, 109.

Celibacy of the clergy, 80.

Chains, 32, 57.

Chambers, R. W., 61, 76, 81, 86, 105, 107, 109; Thomas More, 86, 89, 90, 105, 107, 109.

Change, in ideal commonwealths, 26.

Charles, Prince, later Charles V, 23, 89.

Chaucer, Geoffrey, 17.

Chelsey, More's house at, 35, 59.

Chivalry, its passing, 40.

Choice of profession, in Utopia, 30.

Christendom, divided, 43, 65.

Christian and pagan, 77—80, 82.

Christianity, 49, 72—3, 77, 108.

Church, reform of, 59, 80.

Churches, in Utopia, 53.

Cicero, 8, 17, 29, 38, 92.

Ciceronianus, of Erasmus, 8.

Circulation between town and country, 30.

Cities, in Utopia, 36, 64 sq.

Citizenship, 64.

Civitas Dei, of St. Augustine, 33, 38, 81, 97, 99.

Civitas solis, of Campanella, 4.

Classes, none in Utopia, 29.

Clergy, celibacy of, 80.

Cloth, manufacture of, 19, 57 sq.

Coinage, debasement of, 19.

Colet, John, 41, 43, 78, 82; quoted, 41, 82.

Collins, Churton, ed. Utopia, 86, 88, 90, 94, 101.

Colonies, 35—6, 62; given up, 35, 62.

Colonization, 35—6, 61—3, 65—6, 99, 100, 106; advantages to colonies, 62, 64—5.

Commerce, 39, 64, 65.

Common land agriculture, 57, 74.

Communism, 3, 22, 23, 27, 28, 29, 36, 66, 79; case against, 23, 66—73, 108; case for, 22, 23, 70, 74; conceived as spiri-tual community, 80; in Europe, 74; in Utopia, 29; derived from Plato, 29.

Compulsion, in Utopia, 77.

Confiscation, of land, 11.

Confutation of Tyndale's Answer, of More, 72, 86; quoted, 67—8.

Conquests, 19, 20; case against, 14.

Conscription, in Utopia, 46.

Constitutional treatises, 14.

Contemporary view of Utopia, 81, 109.

Control of government, in Utopia, 37, 58.

Conversation, in Utopia, 36.

Conversion, religious, in Utopia, 49—50.

Convicts, made to work, 13, 19, 29, 30, 31, 58, 94, 108.

Cosmographiae introductio, 27, 89, 91, 94.

Council, in Utopia, 34, 37.

Courtiers, 19—21.

Crafts, in Utopia, 30.
Criminal intention punished, 37.
Criminals condemned to servitude, 13, 19, 29, 30, 31, 58, 94, 108.
Critias, of Plato, 28.
Cromwell, Oliver, 92.
Cure, of evils, 23, 71, 73—4, 83.
Cyrus, 26.

Dante, 99.
De Asse, of Budé, 86.
De Bergerac, Cyrano, 5.
De communione rerum, of Vives, 107; quoted, 72.
De ecclesiae concordia, of Erasmus, 107; quoted 72.
De Gourmont, Gilles, 6.
De lycksaligas ö, of Strindberg, 4.
De orbe novo, of Peter Martyr, 27—8, 94.
De subventione pauperum, of Vives, 86, 89.
De tradendis disciplinis, of Vives, 88, 89, 90, 108.
Decisions, in Council, in Utopia, 37.
Defensive policy, 42—3, 48.
Defoe, Daniel, *Robinson Crusoe*, 4, 7.
Delcourt, Joseph, *Essai sur la langue de Thomas More*, 88.
Delcourt, Marie, 8, 85, 88; ed. *Utopia*, 8, 85, 86, 89.
Den svenska socialismens historia, 85.
Dermenghem, T. M., *More et les utopistes*, 85.
Det landet Victoria, of Topelius, 4.
Dialogue, as a literary form, 15 sq.
Dialogue Concerning Tyndale, of More, 91; quoted, 74, 77.
Dialogue of Comfort, of More, 66, 67, 72, 87, 89, 106, 108, 109; quoted, 66—7, 72—3, 77, 109.
Dice-play, 59.
Dietrich, Ottmar, *Geschichte der Ethik*, 95, 100.
Dietzel, H., *Geschichte des Socialismus*, 85, 98.
Dignity, of man, 50, 76, 107.
Diodorus Siculus, 88.
Disbelief, religious, 59, 104.
Disraeli, Benjamin, Earl of Beaconsfield, 5.
Divorce, 34.
Donner, H. W., *Historisk demonologi*, 91, 100; *Interpretation of Utopia*, 107; *Kristen humanism*, 108; *Machiavellistisk historieskrivning*, 94, 100; *Medeltida förebilder till en internationell fredsorganisation*, 84; *Mores Utopia som samhällsideal*, 84; *Thomas More och samvetets frihet*, 109.
Dream, More's, 1; Utopia, like one, 1—2.
Dress, in Europe, 1; in Utopia, 1, 31, 59.
Dublin Review, 85.
Dubois, Pierre, 99.
Dudok, Gerard, *More and Utopia*, 96.

Earthly paradise, myth of, 28, 103.
Economics, Utopian, 39, 57—8, 64, 97.
Education, 3, 29, 36, 37—8, 52; universal and compulsory, 3, 29, 38.
Edward IV, 99.
Eggs, artificial hatching of, 26—7, 57.
Ekwall, Eilert, 101.
Election, of magistrates, 36—7; of priests, 51.
Ellinger, Georg, 105.
Employment, as cure against crimes, 13, 19.
Enclosures, of land, 11, 19, 57, 87; measures against, 13.
Engels, Friedrich, 3; *Entwicklung des Socialismus*, 85.
England, criticism of, 18; likeness to Utopia, 57, 58, 59, 60, 65, 100, 103; supposed impregnability of, 48, 102.
Englische Studien, 94.
English constitution, 15, 37, 58.
Envy, 42.
Epicurean philosophy, 27, 38, 77, 108.
Epistolae obscurorum virorum, 15.
Equality, of the sexes, 3, 29, 38, 52; social, 59.
Erasmus, Desiderius, 1, 2, 6, 8, 9, 12, 15, 18, 23, 24, 29, 38, 43, 58, 67, 71, 72, 75, 78, 82, 87, 88, 89, 90, 91, 92; *Ciceronianus*, 8; *De ecclesiae concordia*, 107; quoted, 72; *Encomium moriae*, 15, 21, 67, 75; *Epistles*, ed. F. M. Nichols, 84, 109; *Institutio principis Christiani*, 58, 71, 78, 86, 87, 90, 91, 107, 108; quoted, 71, 78, 79; *Opus epistolarum*, ed. P. S. and H. M. Allen, 84, 86, 88, 89, 91, 94, 104, 105; *Paraphrase to the Romans*, 88; translation of Lucian, 88; letters, to Budé, 105; to Hutten, 86, 91, 94, 104, 105; quoted, 24, 29; from Colet, 82; from More, 1, 89, 104.
Erb, Alfons, *Thomas Morus. John Fisher*, 85.
Erewhon, of Butler, 5.
Estate jobbing, 11.
Europe, contrasted with Utopia, 18, 20, 33, 34, 40, 41, 44, 45, 46, 47, 52—3, 54, 55—6, 57—60, 65, 75—6, 78, 79;

similarities with Utopia, 54—5, 56—7, 58—9, 74.

Example, More's manner of teaching by means of, 17, 23, 74, 83.

Exchange, of houses, in Utopia, 31, 81.

Exchange, of people between town and country, 30.

Excommunication, in Utopia, 52.

Expeditionary force, 45 sq.

Experience, 14.

Exports, 30, 39.

Faith and reason, 76—7, 79, 82.

Family, in Utopia, 33, 35, 46, 59.

Feilitzen, C. O. von, 101.

Fetters, 32, 57.

Fines, 19.

Finsk Tidskrift, 91, 100.

Fischer, J., ed. Cosmographiae Introductio, 27, 89, 91, 94.

Fisher, H. A. L., Political History of England, 88.

Flodden, battle of, 102.

Food reserves, 30.

Fools, toleration of, 60.

Forced labour, 29, 30, 31, 58, 108.

Fortescue, Sir John, 12, 48, 69, 86, 88, 90, 102; The Governance of England, 86, 90; quoted, 86, 87.

Fortifications, 42, 46, 48.

Fortnightly Review, 84.

France, foreign policy of, 20.

Freedom, 16; of conscience, 58, 76; of speech, 58; within the law, 38.

Freiland, of Hertzka, 3.

Freund, Michael, Utopia des Thomas Morus, 92, 93, 95, 97, 100, 102, 103, 105, 106.

Froben, John, 6.

Gardens, in Utopia, 31; in West Indies, 28.

Geldner, Ferdinand, 24, 92; Staatsauffassung des Erasmus, 92.

Gems, despised, by More, 1; by Utopians, 32; by West Indians, 27.

Generosity, 39.

Geographical discoveries, 10, 16.

Geometry, 32.

German Catholic attitude to More, 4.

Germania, of Tacitus, 29, 75.

Germans, the, as critics, 23—4, 24—5, 25—6, 31, 55—7, 60—1, 63, 64, 65, 91, 92—3, 95, 97, 98—101, 102, 103, 104, 105 sq., 106, 108; as mercenaries, 20, 53.

Germany and Machiavellian policy, 103.

Gibbins, H. de B., English Social Reformers, 85.

Giles, Peter, 16, 18, 25, 61; letters, to Busleyden, 25, 93; from More, prefatory to Utopia, 25, 56, 89, 93; from More, prefatory to Paris edition, 89, 91.

Glunz, Hans, 80, 109; Shakespeare und Morus, 99, 109.

God, existence of, 50, 77.

Gold and silver, despised, by More, 1; by Utopians, 32, 39, 57, 60; by West Indians, 27; used for fetters, 32, 57; what pots made of, 57.

Golden Age, 28.

Goldsmiths, see Bankers.

Greek, 17; in Utopia, 23, 59, 89; opponents of, 23, 59.

Greek philosophers, Utopians equal to, 32, 102.

Green, John Richard, 88.

Grocyn, William, 33.

Grotius, Hugo, 97.

Gulliver's Travels, of Swift, 4, 7.

Gummerus, Herman, 100.

Gutkelch, A., ed. of Utopia, 85.

Hall, Edward, 88.

Hallett, Philip E., 109; ed. Dialogue of Comfort, 87, 89, 106, 108, 109; ed. Utopia, 86, 89, 90, 91, 96, 104, 107; translation of Stapleton, 87, 105.

Halls, in Utopia, 36.

Handelskrieg, 99—100.

Harington, Sir John, 103; quoted, 49.

Harpsfield, Nicholas, Life of More, 92, 96, 101.

Harrington, James, 4, 97.

Harvest, gathering of, 30.

Heckscher, Eli, 86.

Heidelberger Akademie der Wissenschaften, 91, 98, 99, 100, 101, 103, 104, 105.

Henrikson-Holmberg, G., Socialismen i Sverige, 85.

Henry VII, 37, 58.

Henry VIII, 23, 24, 34, 48, 58, 61, 62, 101, 103.

Herodotus, 105.

Hertzler, J. O., 37, 85; The History of Utopian Thought, 85, 96.

Hertzka, Theodor, 3.

Hirn, Yrjö, 28; Goda vildar och ädla rövare, 94; Ön i världshavet, 85.

Historians, 24—5; their view of Utopia, 3, 23—4.

Historische Vierteljahrschrift, 107.

Historische Zeitschrift, 92.

Historisches Jahrbuch, 98, 100, 106.
Hitchcock, Elsie V., ed. Harpsfield's *Life of More,* 92, 96, 101 ; Roper's *Life of More,* 86, 92, 96, 105, 109.
Hobbes, Thomas, 4, 97.
Holberg. Ludvig, 4.
Hollis, Christopher, *Sir Thomas More,* 89, 108, 109.
Holt, John, letter from More, 84 ; quoted, 2, 32.
Horses, little used in Utopia, 42.
Hospitals, 34.
Hours, of work, 3, 29, 95.
Houses, in Utopia, 31, 36, 60.
Households, in Utopia, 35.
Howells, William Dean, 3.
Huber, E. R., 93, 98, 100, 105 ; quoted, 93, 98.
Huizinga, J., *Erasmus,* 89 ; *Im Bann der Geschichte,* 92, 101.
Humanism, 18, 23, 24, 104 ; achievement of, 8, 15 ; opponents of, 23.
Humanist, satire, 15 ; terminology, 71 ; view of communism, 71—3 ; wit, 9, 26—7.
Hunting, condemned in Utopia, 38.
Husbands, authority of, 34.
Hutten, Ulrich von, letter from Erasmus, 86, 91, 94, 104, 105.
Huvudstadsbladet, 108.
Huxley, Aldous, 4.
Hygiene, 60.
Hythloday, Raphael, 11, 14, 16—17, 18, 19, 20, 21, 22, 23, 24, 25, 26, 32, 33, 39, 54, 57, 58, 60, 67, 69, 70, 71, 74, 82, 91, 92, 94, 105, 107, 108.

Ideal, of More, 78, 108.
Idealism, 108.
Idéenanalyse, 92—3.
Idéengeschichte, 92.
Idleness, not tolerated, 29, 59.
Imitatio Christi, 82.
Immortality, of the soul, 28, 50—1, 59, 77, 104.
Immunity, of the clergy, 59, 104.
Imperfection, of Utopia, 78, 80, 83.
Imports, 39.
Incarnation, the, 80.
Incas, the, 28.
Incubation, artificial, 26—7, 57.
Indemnities, 47.
Independence, of Utopian colonies, 64.
Individualism, 108.
Institutio principis Christiani, of Erasmus, 58, 71, 78, 86, 87, 90, 91, 107, 108 ; quoted, 71, 78, 79.

Intellectuals, in Utopia, 29 sq.
Intention, of *Utopia,* 5, 15, 17 sq., 21, 47 sq., 54, 56, 82—3.
Intention, as bad as crime, 37.
International relations, 41—3, 48—9, 65, 81—2, 98—100, 102, 103, 105.
Interpretation, 25, 67, 72, 77, 79—83.
Iron, lack of, 27, 39.
Isidore, of Seville, 99.
Islands, vulnerable to attack, 48.
Isolation, of Utopia, 98, 103.

Jeu d'esprit, of *Utopia,* 56, 71, 75, 106.
John, of Salisbury, 99.
John III, of Portugal, 90.
Josephson, Ragnar, 101.
Judges, pressure put upon, 19 sq.
Julius II, Pope, 41, 52.
Justice, 46, 59, 63, 82 ; *see also* Law.
Justinian Codex, 9.

Kaegi, Werner, 89.
Karsten, Rafael, *Inkariket,* 89.
Kautsky, Karl, 3. 67, 73, 101, 106 ; *More und seine Utopie,* 84, 88, 101, 106, 107.
King, a good one, 19, 20, 21 ; courts of, 18—19 ; duty of improving, himself, 20, 82 ; the state of his subjects, 19 ; honour of, 13, 58 ; ruler over free men, 99 ; wealth of, 19—20.
Kleinwächter, F., *Staatsromane,* 85.
Kölner anglistische Arbeiten, 99.
Knös, Börje, *Budé,* 86, 87.
Kühn, Johannes, *Morus und Rousseau,* 107.

La grande voyage, of Puaux, 4.
Labour, manual, exemption from, 29 sq. ; forced, 29, 31, 58, 108 ; hours of, 3, 29, 95.
Labourers, hardships of, 12.
Lanceknights, 20, 53.
Land, confiscation of, 11 ; enclosures of, 11, 13, 19, 57, 87.
Lateran Council, 104.
Latin, 7, 17 ; prose, 8.
Latitudinarian theology, 3.
Laurentian style, in Latin, 8.
Laus stultitiae, of Erasmus, *see Moriae encomium.*
Law, rule of, in Utopia, 38, 43, 60, 65, 77 ; Divine, 78 ; international, 41, 42— 3, 46, 63, 64, 98—9, 100, 106 ; man-made, 64, 65, 80, 82 ; of Christ, 77, 80, 82, 108 ; of Moses, 108 ; of nature, 3, 35, 38, 39, 44 sq., 62, 63, 65, 75, 78, 80, 82, 97, 106.
Lawlessness, 76.

Laws, few in Utopia, 38, 97 ; obsolete, 19.

Laws, the, of Plato, 26, 35, 36, 61, 75, 91, 94, 95, 96, 97, 98.

Leadan, I. S., *Domesday of Enclosures,* 87.

Leagues, 41 sq.

Learning, pursuit of, in Utopia, 23, 29 sq., 31—2.

Lectures, 31.

Legality, of redistribution of property, 69.

Legenda aurea, 79.

Leo X, Pope, 104.

Letters and Papers, 88, 104.

Leviathan, of Hobbes, 4.

Libell of Englyshe Polycye, 88.

Lichtenberger, A., *Socialisme utopique,* 85.

Liljegren, S. B., ed. Harrington's *Oceana,* 97.

Lodge, Thomas, quoted, 60.

Logicalia, parva, »the small logicals», 32.

Looking Backward, of Bellamy, 5.

Lovers, 102.

Lucian, 16, 55, 105 ; dialogues translated by More, 16, 88 ; influence of, 5.

Luke, St., 73.

Lupset, Thomas, letter from Budé, 84 ; quoted, 81.

Lupton, J. H., ed. *Utopia,* 84 and passim.

Lutherans, the, 53.

Luxury, 13.

Lytton, Edward Robert Bulwer-Lytton, 1st Earl, 4.

Macauley, Rose, 4.

Machiavelli, Niccolo, 55, 93, 97, 100, 102 ; *Il Principe,* 36, 41, 58, 96, 102.

Machiavellian view of history, 25—6, 57, 94, 97.

Machiavellianism, in Europe, 41, 59, 81 sq., 103.

Mackintosh, Sir James, 105 ; quoted, 56.

Magellan, Ferdinand, 17.

Magistrates, in Utopia, 30, 31, 36—8, 48 —9, 52, 103 sq.

Markets, 36.

Marriages, in Europe, 33, 34 ; in Utopia, 33—4.

Martin, Thierry, 6.

Martyr, Peter, d'Anghiera, 27—8, 31, 51, 75 ; *De orbe novo,* 27, 94.

Marx, Karl, 3, 11.

Materialism, 108.

Matthew, St., 82, 109.

Maundeville, Sir John, *Travels,* 16, 89.

Meals, in Utopia, 36, 59.

Meinecke, Friedrich, 100.

Mercenaries, 13 sq., 19, 40, 44—5, 102, 106.

Michels, V., ed. *Utopia,* 85.

Minos, 26.

Mitigation, of evil, 21—2, 22—3, 24, 74 sq., 82 sq., 86.

Modern Latin literature, 7, 8.

Monastic system, 59, 74, 79.

Money, in ancient Greece, 97 ; in Utopia, 39 ; indifference to, 42.

Monks, in Utopia, 51, 76.

Monopolies, 13, 19.

Month and Catholic Review, 109.

More, Dame Alice, wife to Thomas More, 87.

More, Cresacre, *Life of Thomas More,* 89.

More, John, 61.

More, St. Thomas, *Life,* at Lambeth, 19 ; at Bucklersbury, 15 ; at Chelsea, 35, 59 ; in Parliament, 58 ; ambassador to Flanders, 16 ; career, 89 ; reluctance to enter the court, 18, 23, 24 ; in the Tower, 66 ; lectures on St. Augustine, 33 ; learning, 8—9 ; dream of Utopian princedom, 1 ; his circle, 7 ; death, 43, 82 ; canonized, 3 ; name in Red Army calendar, 3 ; contribution to the English language, 2 ; position in English literature, 7 ;

    Character, adaptability, 24 ; consistency, 67—74 ; faith, 10 ; idiosyncrasies, 59—60 ; optimism, 10, 17 sq. ; intellectual facility, 77, 91, 106 ; irony, 26—7, 39—40, 41, 44, 56, 60 ; Latinity, 8—9 ; manner, 57, 74 ; literary skill, 22—3, 71, 91, 107 ; stranger to ambition, 24 ; attitude to Humanism, 8— 9, 15—16, 18 ; hatred of war, 56, 104 ; views on reform, 13, 22, 61, 71, 74, 79, 80, 82 ; of the Church, 59, 80 ;

    Works, Apology, 68, 71, 82, 90, 91, 95, 106, 107, 109 ; quoted, 68, 109 ; *Confutation of Tyndale,* 72, 86 ; quoted, 67—8 ; *Dialogue Concerning Tyndale,* 91 ; quoted, 74, 77 ; *Dialogue of Comfort,* 66, 67, 72, 87, 89, 106, 108, 109 ; quoted, 66—7, 72—3, 77, 109 ; *English Works,* 24, 86, 87, 88, 89, 91, 104, 107, 108, 109 ; quoted, 67, 74, 77, 87 ; *Epigrams,* 24, 90 ; *Four Last Things,* 89 ; *History of Richard III,* 7, 22, 88, 99 ; in English and Latin, 7 ; *Lucubrationes,* .90 ; *Opera omnia,* 90, 109 ; *Supplication of Souls,* 68 ; *Utopia, see* sub v. ; translation of Lucian, 16, 88 ; of Pico, 18, 23 ; Letters, to Erasmus, 2, 84, 104 ; to

Peter Giles, 89, 91, 104; to John Holt, 84; quoted, 2, 32; to his wife, 87; to Wolsey, 87, 104; from Busleyden, 89.

More, Sir Thomas, as character in the dialogue of *Utopia*, 21, 23, 24, 54, 70, 71, 87.

Morelly, *Naufrage des îles flottantes*, 3.

Moriae encomium, of Erasmus, 15, 21, 67, 75.

Morley, John, *Machiavelli*, 93, 94.

Morris, William, 3, 5; *News from Nowhere*, 5.

Morton, Cardinal, 19, 22, 57, 87; More's character of, 19.

Moses, 26, 108.

Mountjoy, Lord, letter to Erasmus, 86; quoted, 10.

Music, 32.

Narrenschiff, of Brandt, 15.

Natural law, 3, 35, 38, 39, 41 sq., 62, 63, 65, 75, 78, 80, 82, 97, 106.

Natural religion, 3, 49—54, 78.

Naufrage des îles flottantes, of Morelly, 3.

Nazi attitude to More, 3 sq. *Cf. also* Germans, as critics.

New Atlantis, of Bacon, 4, 96.

New world, account of the, 27—8.

News from Nowhere, of Morris, 5.

Nichols, F. M., ed. *The Epistles of Erasmus*, 84, 109.

Niels Klim, of Holberg, 4.

Notes and Queries, 84.

Nusquama, as synonym for Utopia, 2 sq.

Obedience, 34, 58.

Oceana, of Harrington, 4.

Old age, veneration for, 34, 60.

Oligopolium, 9.

Oncken, Hermann, 23, 24, 55—7, 60—1, 63, 73, 88, 91, 93, 94, 95, 98—100, 101, 103, 104, 105, 106; *Introduction*, 91; *Heidelberger Akademie*, 91; quoted, 98—100, 101, 103.

Orphan Island, of Rose Macauley, 4.

O'Sullivan, R., *The Social Theories of Sir Thomas More*, 85.

Overpopulation, 35, 61, 63, 106.

Owen, Robert, 3.

Oxen, used for ploughing, 42.

Oxford English Dictionary, 84; quoted, 2.

»Pacifyer», the, More's name for the author of *A Treatise Concerning the Division between the Spiritualty and the Temporalty*, 1532, attributed by Bale to Christopher Saint-German, 68.

Pagan and Christian, 77—80, 82.

Pandects, the, 9, 109.

Paradoxes, of *Utopia*, 56 sq.

Parliament, in Utopia, 34, 37.

Parliamentary misrule, 37.

Parody, of *Utopia*, 57.

Paul, St., 73.

Peace, plea for, 13—14, 58, 59, 75.

Penal servitude, 13, 19, 29, 30, 31, 58, 94, 108.

Perfection, impossible, 22, 83.

Petrarch, 8.

Phillips, Rowland, Vicar of Croydon, 25, 97.

Philosophers, 17; and Kings, 21.

Philosophy, 21, 32, 38, 78; of More, 108; and Religion, 76—7, 78.

Phylarchs, 36.

Physical training, 42, 47.

Physicians, 34.

Pico della Mirandola, Giovanni, Count, 18, 23, 75, 76, 77, 95, 107; *Adversus astrologos*, 95; *De hominis dignitate*, 108; More's translation of his *Life*, 18, 23.

Plato, 4, 15, 22, 24, 26, 28, 29, 33, 38, 42, 46, 55, 61, 73, 75, 90, 91, 94, 95, 96, 97, 98, 101, 104, 106, 108, 109; *Critias*, 28; *Laws*, 26, 35, 36, 61, 75, 91, 94, 95, 96, 97, 98; *Republic*, 21, 29, 35, 46, 75, 90, 92, 96, 98, 101, 102; *Symposium*, 102; *Timaeus*, 28.

Platonic Academy of Florence, 75.

Platonic element in *Utopia*, 108.

Plautus, 8.

Pleasure, 38, 77.

Pliny, the Elder, 29, 38.

Plutarch, 29.

Poor, the, More's plea for, 12.

Poor Laws, 3.

Political romances, 4.

Pollard, A. F., 11; *Henry VIII*, 88; *Wolsey;* 86, 87, 88.

Polylerites, the, 23, 74, 89, 94, 95, 96, 103.

Pomponazzi, Pietro, 104.

Popes, authority of, 41.

Population, decrease of, 35, 62; increase of, 35, 63; overpopulation, 35, 61, 63, 106.

Populivorus, 9.

Poultry, 26—7, 57.

Poverty, 19, 20, 58, 61; as cause of stealing, 12, 86.

Power, lust for, 65, 81 sq.

Power, E., *Tudor Economic Documents*, 88.
Prayers, in Utopia, 53—4.
Precious metals, despised in Utopia, 32, 39, 57, 60.
Preussische Akademie der Wissenschaften, 101.
Prices, increase in, 13, 19.
Pride, root of vice, 82.
Priests, in Utopia, 51—2; immunity of, 52, 59; marriage of, 52, 80; partaking in war, 52; punishment of, 51 sq.; sanctuary with, 52, 59; women as, 52.
Prince, *see* King.
Prince, the, in Utopia, 34, 36—7; More as, 1.
Prince, the, of Machiavelli, 36, 41, 58, 96, 102.
Privacy, lack of, in Utopia, 31.
Progress, 10, 22.
Property, private, 3, 22—3, 65, 68—73, 99; case against, 22; case for, 23, 68—9; Christianity and, 71—3; redistribution of, 68—71.
Prosperity, 13.
Puaux, René, 4.
Public spirit, of the Humanists, 18, 89.
Punishment, 52; capital, 12 sq., 31, 47, 79, 87; gradation of, 30 sq., 59.

Quintilian, 8.

Rabelais, François, 5.
Racial theory, 64.
Ralegh, Sir Walter, 102.
Rastell, John, 61, 62.
Ravaging, in war, 13, 47, 87 sq.
Reading lesson at dinner, 59.
Reason, Utopia founded on, 49, 76.
Reason and faith, 76—7, 79, 82.
Rebels, 65.
Reform, 3, 13, 22, 59, 61, 71, 74, 79, 80, 82.
Religion, diversity of, 49, 50, 80; natural, 3, 49—54, 78; the Utopian, 49—54.
Religion and philosophy, 76—7.
Remus, 26.
Renaissance literature, 7.
Renaissance princes, 23.
Reparations, 47.
Republic, the, of Plato, 21, 29, 35, 46, 75, 90, 92, 96, 98, 101, 102.
Restrictions, on religious freedom, 50.
Reuchlin, Johann, 75.
Rhenanus, Beatus, 109.
Rich men, duty of, 72—3; More's severity on, 13, 19.

Richard III, 99.
Richard III, History of, by More, 7, 22, 88, 99.
Ritter, Gerhard, 24, 25, 64, 91, 93, 94, 97, 98, 100, 101, 103, 105, 106; *Machtstaat und Utopie,* 91, 92, 93, 94, 97, 98, 100, 101, 103, 104, 105, 106; quoted, 56, 57, 64, 93; translation of *Utopia,* 88, 91.
Robinson Crusoe, of Defoe, 4, 7.
Robinsonian fiction, 5.
Robynson, Ralph, translator of *Utopia,* 6, 7, 9, 97.
Rome, ancient, 31, 105.
Rome, sack of, 53.
Romulus, 26.
Roper, William, *Life of More,* 86, 92, 96, 105, 109.
Routh, E. M. G., *More and his Friends,* 84.
Ruskin, John, 3.
Rydberg, Victor, 26, 94.

Sampson, G., ed. of *Utopia,* 85.
Sanctions, 42—3, 64, 65.
Sanctuary, 52, 59.
Sargent, Daniel, *Thomas More,* 109.
Satire, 15—16, 17, 39—40, 44—5, 56, 57, 101.
Scholarship, degradation of, 101.
Schoman, Emilie, *Französische Utopisten,* 85.
School philosophy, 21.
Schoolmen, 8, 15.
Science, 32.
Scots, the, 20.
Seebohm, F., *The Oxford Reformers,* 97, 108.
Selfishness, root of vice, 81 sq.
Seneca, 17.
Serfs, 29, 30—1, 38, 94, 106.
Servants, dismissal of, 13, 87; great number of, 13, 19.
Service, ideal of, 38.
Servitude, 29, 47, 78, 79, 95, 108.
Sexes, equality of, 3, 29, 38, 52.
Shakespeare, 48.
Sheep, increased rearing of, 11, 13, 19.
Shepherd, the king as, 20.
Ships, sailed in by Hythloday, 17.
Sick, nursing of the, 34; the incurably sick, 34 sq.
Slaves, *see* Bondmen.
Social distinctions, in Utopia, 29.
Social reform, 13.
Social reformers, 3.
Socialism, 3.

Socialist view of Utopia, 3.
Sociologist view of Utopia, 3, 79.
Sociology, 3.
Socrates, 21.
Sombart, Werner, 101.
Soul, immortality of, 28, 50—1, 59, 77, 104.
Specula principis, 14, 21, 58, 90 sq.
Spies, 47.
Spirits, of the departed, 51.
Staatsromane, 4, 5.
Stapleton, Thomas, 6; *Tres Thomae*, 87, 105.
Stealing, causes of, 12, 86; cure against, 13, 31.
Stein, L. von, *Geschichte der socialen Bewegung*, 85.
Sternberg, Kurt, *Utopia des Thomas Morus*, 95, 98, 100, 102, 105, 108.
Stoics, 35.
Stoic element in *Utopia*, 108.
Streets, in Utopian cities, 36, 60.
Strindberg, August, 4.
Studies, in Utopia, 23, 29 sq., 31—2.
Sturge, Charles, *Tunstall*, 87.
Suicide, 34.
Supplication of Souls, of More, 68.
Surplus production, 30, 39.
Svenning, C. E., translation of *Utopia*, 85.
Svenska Dagbladet, 94, 101, 109.
Swift, Jonathan, 4; *Gulliver*, 4, 7.
Symposium, of Plato, 102.
Cyphogrants, 36—7.

Tacitus, 9, 29, 75, 102; *Germania*, 29, 75.
Taft, I. A., ed. *Apology of Sir Thomas More*, 90, 91, 95, 106, 107, 109.
Tawney, R. H., *Tudor Economic Documents*, 88.
Taylor, Helen, *More on the Politics of To-Day*, 84.
Terence, 8.
The Coming Race, of Lytton, 4.
The Governance of England, of Fortescue, 12, 86, 90, 102; quoted, 86, 87.
Thieves, punishment of, 13, 31.
Thomas Aquinas, St., 13, 77, 90.
Thrasymachus, in Plato's *Republic*, 21.
Times, the, quoted, 84.
Toleration, religious, 50, 80, 109.
Topelius, Zachris, 4.
Toys, 32.
Trade relations, interruption of, 42 sq.
Tranibores, 36—7.
Travel, tales of, 16.
Treaties, 41 sq.

Trevelyan, G. M., *English Social History*, 88.
Truce, 47.
Trusteeship, of Utopians, 65.
Tunstall, Cuthbert, 2.
Tyndale, William, 67, *Answer to More's Dialogue*, 106.
Tyranny, 37, 42, 58, 65, 76, 99.
Tyrant, defined, 99.

Udepotia, as synonym for Utopia, 3.
Ullrich, Hermann, *Robinsonaden*, 85.
Unemployment, 61.
Unity, of More's thought, 108.
Ur-Utopia, 98.
Utilitarian philosophy, 3.
Utility, of redistribution of property, 69.
Utopia, of More, editions, 6, 61, 85; Collins, 86, 88, 90, 94, 101; Delcourt, 8, 85, 86, 89; Hallett, 86, 89, 90, 91, 96, 104, 107; Lupton, 84 and passim; Michels and Ziegler, 85; Sampson and Gutkelch, 85; translations, 6, 7, 61, 85; Ritter, 88; Svenning, 85; dedication, 61; prefatory letter to Peter Giles, 89, 104; second prefatory letter, 89, 91; commendary epistles, 6, 88; commentaries, 8, 10, 85, 86; criticism, 6, 9—10, 54—7, 60—3, 73, 98—100, 101—2, 103, 104, 105, 106, 108;
  characterization of, 1—2, 10, 22, 38, 54, 63, 82—3, 93; as programme of reform, 5, 23—4; as source of our knowledge of the period, 14 sq; application to the problems of the day, 58, 61, 65—6, 71, 74, 79; the period, 10; sources, 8—9, 27—9, 77; faithfulness to sources, 33, 38, 101, 108; scholarship, 75, 93, 101, 108; summary of pagan customs and philosophy, 75, 93, 108;
  as entertainment, 5; form, 16; composition, 6, 9, 55—6, 61, 63, 98; style, 5, 7, 8—9; artistic merits, 6, 17; descriptive power, 4, 25; grammar, 9; vocabulary, 8—9.
  elements of thought, 108; ideal contents, 5, 7, 8; purpose, 5, 15, 17 sq., 21, 47 sq., 56, 82—3; moralizing features, 33; interpretation, 6, 11, 25, 26, 33, 77, 79, 82—3; difficulties, 60—75; its appeal to all, 83;
  topical interest, 11; influence, 3—6; literary, 4, 5, 6; social, 3, 5; summary, 82—3.
Utopia, name, 2—3, 84; situation, 25; turned into island, 26; climate, 30;

soil, 30 ; production, 29—30, 39 ; population, 29 ; character of inhabitants, 11, 23, 38, 39 ;

states, 39, 60 ; administration, 36—7 ; government, 37 ; society, 11 sq., 29, 39, 77 ; economics, 39, 57—8, 64, 97 ; industries, 30 sq. ; trade, 39 ; foreign, 39, 64 ; exports, 30, 39 ; imports, 39 ; foreign policy, 40—1, 42—3, 47—9, 63—6, 98—100, 104, 106 ; colonial policy, 35, 60—3, 64—5, 99, 100, 106 ; advantages to colonies, 62, 64—5 ; warfare, 39—48, 54—5, 101, 105, 106 ;

families, 33, 35, 46, 59 ; professions, 30 ; dress, 31 ; cities, 36 ; houses, 31, 36 ; gardens, 31 ;

education, 3, 29, 36, 37 sq., 42, 52 ; studies, 31—2, 38 ; religion, 49—54.

Utopian, meaning of the word, 2.

Utopian romance, characterization of, 5.

Utopians, 11, 23, 29—54, 55, 57, 59, 60, 63, 64, 65 ; generous, 39 ; helpful, 38 ; law-abiding, 63—4, 65, 69 ; peaceloving, 40—1 ; reasonable, 27 ; their idealism, 76 ; Epicureans, 38 ; their place in the development of civilization, 75, 78, 93.

Utopus, King, 26, 50.

Vagabonds, 13.

Vahlen, Theodor, 100.

Valla, Laurentius, 8.

Vanity, 81.

Vapensmeden, of Victor Rydberg, 26, 94.

Vennerström, I., *Svenska utopister,* 85.

Vergangenheit und Gegenwart, 100.

Vernacular literatures, 7.

Vespucci, Amerigo, 16, 17, 24, 27, 31, 32, 33, 34, 38, 39, 46, 47, 53, 61, 75 ; *Voyages,* 27, 31, 34 ; *see also Cosmographiae introductio.*

Violation of justice, 63—4.

Virtues, Christian and pagan, 81.

Vision, of *Utopia,* 2, 79.

Vives, Juan Luis, 12, 38, 72, 79, 88, 89, 90 ; *De communione rerum,* 107 ; quoted, 72 ; *De subventione pauperum,* 86, 89 ; *De tradendis disciplinis,* 88, 89, 90, 108 ; plan for the studies of Princess Mary, 88.

Volunteers, 45 sq.

Vorländer, Karl, 100 ; *Von Machiavelli bis Lenin,* 85, 100.

Voyage en Icarie, of Cabet, 3.

Waldseemüller, Martin, 27, 89 ; *Cosmographiae introductio,* 27, 89, 91, 94.

Walter, H., ed. Tyndale's *Answer to More's Dialogue,* 106.

War, 35, 39—48, 61, 65, 76, 90, 99—101, 102, 105, 106 ; argument against, 43, 48 ; causes of, 13—14, 35, 42—3, 62, 63, 99—100 ; Plato on, 46, 101 sq., 106 ; West Indians and, 27, 46.

Wards, in Utopian cities, 36.

Warner, Sir G., ed. *Libell of Englyshe Polycye,* 88.

Wars of the Roses, 11, 22.

Watson, F., *Vives: On Education,* 88, 89, 90, 107, 108.

Wealth, of the people, 13, 58 ; unequal distribution of, 11.

Wells, H. G., 2, 4 ; *A Modern Utopia,* 4 ; *An Englishman Looks at the World,* 84 ; *Outline of History,* 85.

West Indies, account of, 27—8.

Wieser, F. von, ed. *Cosmographiae introductio,* 27, 89, 91, 94.

Wikman, K. Rob. V., 95.

Wit, 9, 26—7.

Wolsey, Cardinal, 13, 58, 87, 90 ; More's letter to, 87, 104.

Women, education for, 29 ; professions for, 30 ; partaking in war, 27, 46.

Wool, industry and trade, 19, 57 sq.

Work, as cure against crimes and unemployment, 13, 19, 58, 61 ; hours of, 3, 29, 95.

World, wretchedness of the, 22.

Worship, in Utopia, 49, 53 sq.

Wriothesley, Charles, 88.

Xenophon, 90.

Xerxes, 94.

Zapoletes, the, 44—5, 46, 56.

Zeitschrift für die gesamte Staatswissenschaft, 93.

Ziegler, Th., ed. of *Utopia,* 85.